STRAIGHT ROWS

The Deimler Barn

STRAIGHT ROWS

Stories of Growing Up on a Farm
During the Great Depression

Thomas R. Deimler, Sr

TenPenniesFarm Publishing
Smyrna, GA

ISBN 13: 978-0-692-50584-7

For inquiries, contact Tom Deimler: tomdeimler@me.com

Book design by Adam Robinson for Good Book Developers

I wish to express my deep appreciation to my parents William and Emma Deimler, my grandmother Kathryn Deimler and my one-room school teacher Miss Alice Demey for helping me become the person I am today.

Contents

A Psalm of Life

by Henry Wadsworth Longfellow

What the Heart of the Young Man
Said to the Psalmist.

Tell me not, in mournful numbers,
Life is but an empty dream!
For the soul is dead that slumbers,
And things are not what they seem.

Life is real! Life is earnest!
And the grave is not its goal;
Dust thou art, to dust returnest,
Was not spoken of the soul.

Not enjoyment, and not sorrow,
Is our destined end or way;
But to act, that each to-morrow
Find us farther than to-day.

Art is long, and Time is fleeting,
And our hearts, though stout and brave,
Still, like muffled drums, are beating
Funeral marches to the grave.

In the world's broad field of battle,
In the bivouac of Life,
Be not like dumb, driven cattle!
Be a hero in the strife!

Trust no Future, howe'er pleasant!
Let the dead Past bury its dead!
Act,— act in the living Present!
Heart within, and God o'erhead!

Lives of great men all remind us
We can make our lives sublime,
And, departing, leave behind us
Footprints on the sands of time;

Footprints, that perhaps another,
Sailing o'er life's solemn main,
A forlorn and shipwrecked brother,
Seeing, shall take heart again.

Let us, then, be up and doing,
With a heart for any fate;
Still achieving, still pursuing,
Learn to labor and to wait.

PREFACE

I LIVED ON A FARM IN THE LATTER YEARS OF THE GREAT Depression. I've always wanted to tell the story, and here it is in my own words.

This writing is an accounting that reflects the best way to ensure my family will get a true picture of my early life. The book consists of a series of vignettes describing experiences that took place on our own farm. Within these pages, the story defines the hardships and the successes, the unpleasant and the fun, the mundane and the exciting—all true, as I know the truth.

The early farmer who had to plow the field and plant corn using mules and then a tractor prided himself in having straight rows. Sometimes they even compared how much straighter theirs were than the neighbor next door. They taught their sons to plow by fixing their eye on a firm object on the other side on the field such as a rock, tree or fence post. Look straight ahead they said and never look back.

My parents believed in the straight row method of plowing and planting. We were told this is the only way when the tomato field was designed with a measuring tape and corner stakes. The area was geometric and the seedling plants in rows evenly spaced.

By the sweat of their brow, the brawn of their body, and with a mindset of perfection, a family was forged that defines each of us many years later. But growing plants was a whole lot more than perfect rows. The teachings of farming guided me in the right path and I learned much about life in the process.

This book, *Straight Rows*, will tell you how it was, cause you some sadness, make you laugh, and excite you. It will for certain enlighten you about a lifetime gone by and give new insight to a culture vanished forever.

Tom Deimler
August 2015

INTRODUCTION

THIS IS A STORY OF A TIME IN HISTORY THAT WE SHALL NEVER see again. It is about a young man who, along with his older brother and younger sister, grew up on a farm in Pennsylvania during the 1930's, until he left in 1952 to enter college.

His young parents moved there to take over the farming operation from his dad's father and mother. The great depression of the late 1920's still had a major grip on a country struggling to grow and modernize. Even so, they had left behind good jobs in order to accept the farming responsibility.

A large portion of the population was still on the farm at that time, so their endeavors were in the mainstream of the lifestyle of those days. The emphasis was on growing crops both for their own needs and to sell for their primary income.

Folks were mostly very poor and had very few material belongings.

Farming was not easy, with the entire family being involved in the planting, cultivating and harvesting process. Everyone had a job to do and it was very much a team effort.

During this time period, the country was evolving from the depression. Living in homes without central heat or bathrooms was quite common. Cooking on a wood-fired stove in the winter gave warmth to the kitchen which was the common focal point of most farm homes. Some farms had a summer kitchen where kerosene stoves were used for cooking. Livestock and poultry grain and mash feed was purchased in floral and other prints. It was usual practice to make bed sheets, tea towels, and tablecloths from this cotton material. The young man of our story's grandmother did most of the sewing at a foot-power machine in the upstairs hallway.

World War II began on December 7, 1941. During the next four years, the country took on a new role as everyone rallied around the war effort. This farm, like the others, was important to the war effort in providing food for the military and overall population.

Beyond 1945, the economy began to recover and life became just a bit easier. Tilling the soil with horses and walking behind the plow was phasing out. Those who could afford to do so, purchased tractors and other more current equipment. Our first tractor was purchased about that time. Farms began to install heating, water, electricity, indoor toilets and bathrooms.

The hard work was still there and gleaming a life from the soil remained a family business. There was little time for play, but recreation was carved out for occasional fun activities.

Following the end of the war, there was yet another change in rural life. The home construction business was flourishing and people were moving to town. The country was booming and things that were rationed or scarce previously were becoming plentiful. Life continued to get better for most people. As always, it was all about working together. Some farmers were beginning to look at other ways to provide for their families. Jobs outside the farm were more plentiful and many of the children, as they grew up, were looking at an education after high school and careers beyond the farm.

Out of this formative lifestyle came the next generation ready to assume important roles in their community. The lessons of the land were firmly a part of who they were, defining them as strong, hard working and committed individuals.

FAMILY TREE

Thomas Richard Deimler

Paternal Grandparents

Isaac Ober Deimler, born October 5, 1871 in Dauphin County, PA; died, January 29, 1938

Kathryn M. Kreiser, born March 29, 1875 in Dauphin County, PA; died December 25, 1951

Maternal Grandparents

Charles Ervin Meinsler, born January 28, 1887 in Dauphin County, PA; died January 22, 1967

Kathryn Pearl Kohr, born February 19, 1891 in Dauphin County, PA; died May 12, 1961

Parents

William LeRoy Deimler (Bill), born January 10, 1909 in Dauphin County, PA, He was the youngest of six children, having two brothers and three sisters; died December 17, 1987 in Alamogordo, NM

Emma Mae Meinsler Deimler, born April 26, 1909 in Royalton, Dauphin County, PA. Emma was the oldest of six children, having two sisters and three brothers; died August 30, 1995 in Alamogordo, NM

Marriage: Bill and Emma were married on September 23, 1928 in Royalton, PA in the home where they were setting up housekeeping. Witnesses were both parents.

Children of Emma and Bill

William LeRoy Deimler, Jr., born August 27, 1932 in Lower Swatara Township, Dauphin County, PA. Married Ella Marie Walter, December 25, 1953 in Baltimore, MD; born November 9, 1934 in Granville, PA

Thomas Richard Deimler, born June 29, 1934 in Lower Swatara Township, Dauphin County, PA. Married Shirley Ann Swisher, on Nov 22, 1958 in St. Paul's United Methodist Church, Elizabethtown, Lancaster County, PA; born March 11, 1935

Peggy Ann Deimler, born Jan 22, 1937 in Harrisburg, Dauphin County, PA. Married George Trumbull Weimer, Jr. on June 30, 1956 in Middletown, PA; born December 23, 1933 in Washington, DC; died Feb 13, 2010

Children of Tom and Shirley

Thomas Richard Deimler, Jr., born Sep 9, 1959 in Harrisburg, Dauphin County, PA. Married Sherry Lynn Jones September 26, 1986 in Jacksonville, NC; born April 8, 1962; Married Joycita Zambrano on April 15, 2000 in Chapel Hill, NC; born August 23, 1972

Stephen Jay Deimler, born November 9, 1961 in Hagerstown, MD; married Rita Ann Stancavage October 31, 1998 in Chapel Hill, NC; born Jul 23, 1969 in Pottsville, PA

Michael Scott Deimler, born September 29, 1964 in Baltimore, MD. Married Dian Elizabeth Sokolowski, Aug 8, 1987 in Gastonia, Gaston County, NC; born December 16, 1962 in Champaign, IL

Grandchildren

Children of Tom Jr and Sherry Lynn Jones

Alexandra Grace Deimler, born August 8, 1989 in Jacksonville, NC

Thomas Richard Deimler III, (Trey) born June 20, 1994 in Durham Regional Hospital, Durham County, NC

Children of Tom Jr and Joycita

Enrique Zambrano Swisher Armando Deimler born August 7, 2008 in Cincinnati, OH

Cruz Noah Zambrano Deimler born December 31, 2012 in Folsom, CA

Daughter of Joycita: **Arielle Mae Welch** born December 20, 1989

Children Of Mike and Dian

Jacob Michael Deimler born September 6, 1989 in University Of Pennsylvania Hospital, Philadelphia

Jessica Rose Deimler born April 25, 1992 in Boston, MA

Parented by Mike and Dian: **Jeffrey Connell** born October 15, 1989, Atlanta, GA

Great Granddaughter

Ella Lee Ann Albertson born July 29, 2014 in Chapel Hill, NC; daughter of Alexandra Grace Deimler Albertson and Ian Albertson, married October 19, 2013

Side view of Deimler barn and Bill

STRAIGHT ROWS

Dad plowing straight rows

THE FARM

AROUND 1930, DAD ACQUIRED THE FARM FROM HIS father, Isaac Deimler for about $3000. The land we owned consisted of twenty three acres which included a house, garage, barn and several poultry buildings. Mom worked alongside Dad to run the farm, and my brother, sister, and I had daily chores to perform. The farm was located in central Pennsylvania, Route 441, near Middletown. My older brother, Bill, and I were born on the farm while my younger sister, Peggy, was born in Polyclinic Hospital in Harrisburg. We lived there through our high school years. It was here that I learned the value of hard work. I was taught that anything worth doing was worth doing right.

My Grandpa Deimler, Isaac Ober Deimler, passed away in 1938, at age 67 when I was only three and one half years old. He was not a direct influence in my life. However, I am told by my parents the he often held me on his knee, and occupied me playfully when Mom was busy with other work.

It is important to mention that his imprint was obvious on our farm. He was a hard worker and set the pace for the daily chores. As the original owner, he helped to construct many of the poultry buildings and a pig pen addition to the barn. Isaac was very progressive for his time. He installed a wind generator which charged batteries. This provided electricity for the house, barn and other buildings. Later on, he and two neighbors, Isaac Coble and Horace Strayer, built a power line from Middletown to provide electricity to their farms.

Grandpa and Dad constructed a large two-floor chicken house to raise layers for egg production and broilers for butchering. The chicken house was equipped with electric brooders and a furnace to provide hot water heat. He borrowed on his life insurance to pay for these and later paid it back. It is interesting to note that the chickens lived in a more modern setting than the family. Home improvements came at a later time when additional funds became available.

In that very rural area of Pennsylvania, we were isolated from the world. Our nearest friends were a couple miles away on a neighboring farm. Bicycles were our primary mode of transportation until age sixteen when we got our drivers license. My brother and I often biked to a friend's house, either Harry or Junie. Both were about our age. These visits were most often on a Sunday afternoon, our weekly break from work.

All three of us kids went to elementary school in a nearby one-room schoolhouse where we had the same teacher throughout our first eight years of formal education. On most days, we walked the one mile distance to and from school. In the evening, the students formed a line to walk along the edge of the road. The student living the farthest away was the safety patrol leader and the closest was at the end.

Farming requires a strong family. It must be one that works together to get the job completed. Ours was a meager lifestyle with very little except for the bare necessities. It was a "hardscrabble life," but I never knew I was poor!

The kitchen was the heartbeat of all that happened on the farm. Mom cooked on a wood stove, which was also the source of heat in the cold winter months. At harvest time, at least twelve people were crammed around the dining table. My grandmother often was the chief cook because my mom was out working the farm with my dad. Neighbors, hired workers, family—everyone gathered and enjoyed a large meal and the work at hand. Meals on the farm tended to be satisfying and could include scrapple, pudding or sausage for breakfast; fried chicken, pork chops, ham or hog maul at lunch or dinner. Scrapple was a gelled meat that Mom or Grandma fried. Pudding wasn't sweet at all, but a delicacy made from ground and boiled meat, which included the bones, head and organ meats. Nothing went to waste on the farm.

Because all three daily meals were cooked on the big, rustic wood stove, the kitchen stayed quite warm and our family tended to gather here. Rising heat from the stove rose through a vent to the second floor which heated the bedroom I shared with my brother, Bill. In the hot months of summer we did not cook in the kitchen nor spend as much time there. Instead, the summer kitchen, which we called the "shed", became an area of much activity. Mom had a kerosene stove here where she did all the cooking during June to September and canned everything we grew which included making her own sauerkraut, ketchup and many different kinds of jams and jellies, and she even cured ham.

Behind the rocker near the wood stove in the kitchen was a large woodbox that had to be filled every day. My first task each afternoon, upon returning home from school, was to split the wood into just the right size to fit into the kitchen stove opening. Logs were cut in the summer by Dad and stored in a large woodshed with a roof that kept them dry. After splitting the wood, I hauled it in a wheel barrow from the wood shed about a hundred or more yards from the house.

On the back porch was an "ice box" refrigerator. The cooling method was quite effective as the large block of ice, which accounted for one third of the inside space, kept our food cold. One of the highlights as a child was the twice weekly arrival of the "ice-man". He drove a truck about the size of a dump truck. On it was loaded very large pieces of ice covered with heavy tarps for insulation. He knew the exact size to cut then separated a chunk from the main piece very quickly with an ice pick. The exciting part for us was all of the little slivers of ice from the cutting—ours for the taking. We would gather hands full! Boy were those refreshing on a hot summer day!

Until I was eight, there was no running water in the house except for one faucet and a small sink in the kitchen. A "bath" might consist of huddling around the kitchen sink with wash cloth, soap and towel. In the summer we bathed outside in a galvanized tub, or sometimes in the shed. I don't remember being modest, which I guess was a good thing! Our toilet was an outside "two-holer," as they were called. Making the trek to this antique structure was a shivering experience on a cold winter's night in January, especially with a two foot deep blanket of snow covering the ground. Regular "tissue" was very rare but the old seed catalogs served us well.

Dad was past the age eligible to have joined the military to fight in World War II, so instead he worked at the nearby Air Force Base in Middletown. Money became a little more plentiful and at last there were enough funds to install a furnace and bath. Sometime in the early nineteen forties, when I was about eight years old, a radiator heating system was finally installed. The coal fuel for the large coal furnace was delivered on a dump truck and came into the basement on a metal chute which dumped into a large storage bin. Dad shoveled the coal into the furnace every morning and evening all winter long. Our first bathroom with running water, including toilet, tub and shower, also was installed at this time.

The farmhouse was large enough that it supported private quarters for my grandparents who helped run the farm until they passed. It had a total of eleven rooms, three porches and two large walk-in closets on the second floor. A gigantic attic was on the third floor where many interesting relics were stored. Although they had their own small kitchen and dining room, Grandma and Grandpa still ate many meals with us, especially during harvest time when my grandmother did most of the cooking. Close to their porch door was what we called the "Bosh." This was a German word that described a water cistern. The rain spouts were directed to this water-proofed cistern and my grandmother dipped water from it to wash her clothing as well as her hair.

The two-story garage housed the pickup truck and a large upstairs workshop with every tool imaginable. The garage bays were mostly used for slaughtering and preparing turkeys and chickens, either for our personal use or for sale.

Two mules, one or two cows and a couple of calfs lived in the bottom level of the barn. A barnyard joined that part of the barn, and was large enough for the animals to exercise daily. Large piles of manure from cleaning their stalls each day occupied a part of that area. This was later forked into a manure spreader and hauled into the fields.

There was also enough space for a large storage room in the bottom level corner of the barn that housed our annual potato crop. This room was partially underground as the barn itself sat on the lower side of a small hill. The walls were insulated with plastic, and the window was also sealed. Potatoes like a cool temperature, but temperatures below freezing meant they would spoil or rot.

Hay and straw for the animals, as well as grain and mash for the poultry, were stored on the second floor of the barn. There was an opening through which to pass the hay and straw into the lower level. I forked hay and straw down the open chute each day. The very heavy weight of the second-floor stores strained the sturdy beams. We raised all of the hay, straw, corn and wheat ourselves for the animals and poultry, with it just lasting until spring. A storage area that housed cultivators, extra farm equipment and a long pig pen were attached to the barn. Six living areas each housed four pigs for a total of twenty four pigs at any given time. As soon as the pigs were sold at market, the pens were cleaned and readied for the next herd.

Rats, mice and English sparrows were the main culprits of disease and damage on the farm to both livestock and cash crops. The sparrows carried a disease—blackhead—to which turkeys were very susceptible and resulted in high mortality rate in both chickens and turkeys. Birds would fly into the pens and eat grain from the feeders, passing the disease through contaminated feed. Rats also carried disease, but mostly chewed holes in grain and mash bags and would eat in the grain bins. Dad did not use any form of poison to rid these pests so my brother and I were paid five cents per killed rat and a penny for mice and sparrows.

Cats were also vital in the reduction of rodents. Like all of us, they earned their keep. The number of cats we had always varied and actually a count was never kept. There was one cat we named Mama who was always near the back porch. Daily she would proudly display her kills from the previous evening. Every morning there would be a rat skin turned inside out in plain sight for all to admire.

Dad rented about fifteen acres from Mrs. Mildred Strayer, a neighbor just across the road. Here, we planted many vegetables for the farmer's market and Mom's peddle route. We farmed "for the half"—that is, sharing expenses and dividing the harvest—about forty acres owned by Grant Auch, father of my Aunt Dot, my mom's sister-in-law.

Our own twenty three acres was largely a vegetable farm with nearly every variety of vegetable. Five hundred peach trees in an orchard accompanied by a few cherry trees rounded out the growing season. In the late winter, pruning the peach trees was a major job. Dad did the cutting and Bill and I gathered the loose branches and hauled them to the brush pile for burning. Mom drove our pickup truck loaded with fruit and vegetables to the farmer's market on Saturdays, did her peddle route door-to-door, and her wholesale route to the grocery stores in the nearby community of Middletown each twice a week.

Each year we raised about 1,200 turkeys for the Thanksgiving, Christmas and New Years market. This required several large turkey pens that were constructed about five feet above the ground so as to keep their feet off of soil that may have been contaminated by chickens. Keeping them healthy made turkeys a challenge to grow.

A large double floor chicken house was for our layers and accommodated about 1,000 female chickens. Each year 300 baby chicks arrived. Dad only kept the layers for three years and in the spring the oldest laying chickens were sold for butchering. The chicks were initially put into empty pens and in the summer were moved out on a grass field. They ranged there until frost at which time they would start laying eggs. Structures built in A-frame style with open sides and ends housed them during this period. The chickens ran free during the day and returned to the small range houses with doors closed at night. They were later moved to the main chicken building where our family had worked together to make sure it was cleaned thoroughly. Lime was spread to help keep the floors and roost area dry and to control disease. The dirt and lime made this a dusty job and I ended with coughing and watering eyes.

It was my job to take care of the chickens on a daily basis which included feeding and gathering of the eggs. Working in the shed, Grandmother checked every egg for cracks and dirt, and carefully spot-cleaned them with a wet cloth. The eggs left in a wire basket were then carried to the main basement where they were packed to be sold. Dad carefully graded them into large, medium and small sizes. He did most of it by sight but often used a scale to double check. Egg production was our only year-round "cash crop," and the egg retailer picked them up at the farm twice a week paying upon receipt of the eggs.

DAD

D AD WAS A VERY INDUSTRIOUS AND DEDICATED FARMER. After high school graduation, he and Mom married. Both had jobs with potential careers of their own. Dad had been working for American Food Store and was already promoted to assistant manager. Mom had a good position as a secretary-typist. Their life was taking positive shape.

Grandma and Grandpa Deimler had three sons and Dad was the youngest. They wanted one of them to buy and take over the farming operation. The offer to purchase the farm had been given to the older sons first, but that possibility had not worked out because the rigors of farming were more than they and their family desired. When it was presented to Dad and Mom as an option, they said yes. A major change in their lives began.

Having very limited funds, it was not an easy move financially. The farm purchase was set up as a loan to be paid over a period of time as income permitted. Also, farming was a new lifestyle for Mom so many adjustments were necessary. Of course, this all added stress to Dad's life as he wanted so badly for it to be a success.

Dad taught me a lot, but the one thing with the most influence on me is that, "hard work never hurt anyone and is a mighty fine characteristic." I have never known a harder worker than my Dad. Being of German origin, he organized his plan for the day precisely and then proceeded to accomplish it. It was a daylight-to-dark endeavor. His expectation, not only for himself, but for all who worked with him, including his family, was perfection, and his ability to tolerate anything less was very limited. There were times that he got extremely angry when you may not have done the job at his high standards. There was no doubt of how well you did as he shouted loudly. At times like this, I often felt quite sad and wondered if I would ever measure up to his mark of excellence.

I recall that on Sunday afternoons, just when we wanted a break, Dad's mind was still working. We often sat in the shade of a large oak tree in the backyard enjoying the afternoon breezes. Dad described in detail each day of the coming week and assigned various projects to each of us. I must admit that this was a bit irritating to the rest of the family, but Dad was very much in charge.

Dad approached farming in an interesting manner. For example, the tomato patch was laid out like a formal garden with every row straight. Each tomato plant was supported with a tobacco lath, a thin wooden stake used to hang tobacco in drying barns. The tomatoes were tied to the stick, and the plants were suckered so that only the main stem remained. In this manner, the harvest produced much larger tomatoes. Cultivating the tomatoes was a two-person project. I led one of our mules down the row with Bill behind the cultivator. We grew about three acres, so it could be considered one of our major summer crops.

Preparation of the late winter seed beds was a task that Dad reserved for himself. He raised the planting areas just off the ground and covered them with what we called hot bed sash. Preparing the soil was intensive labor. Dad really loved the earth and he showed it in this process. He built a large sieve about five feet high and framed with two by four lumber. The open area was covered with a fine mesh wire with half-inch openings. Dad shoveled the rich topsoil against the wire sieve and only the fine dirt passed though. He continued this process tirelessly until the ground beneath the sieve was of the finest quality. The soil was then placed into the hot beds and seeds were planted. We raised a lot of our plants from seed, but the one I remember the most are sweet potatoes. This crop was the smaller variety of Jersey Sweets and the little vines, when ready in the spring, were pulled from the bed and transplanted in the mounded rows in the field.

Crating the eggs was also Dad's priority so as to be ready for the weekly pickup. He spent considerable time making certain the eggs were properly packaged The eggs were placed in cases made from ultra thin slices of wood. The case had two separate compartments with five layers of eggs in each. The individual eggs were protected with cardboard dividers so that each compartment had about eighteen eggs, and each case had fifteen dozen eggs. Our farm crops were mostly seasonal so the weekly egg money was critical to our cash flow.

A large harvest of Irish potatoes came in early fall around September. We used a horse-drawn digger machine with a plow-type blade to unearth them, and later on used a tractor to of this work. The potatoes passed through a shaker to remove the soil before dropping out the back onto the field. At that point, we picked them up by hand and loaded them onto a farm wagon. From there, they were hauled to the barn storage area. The potato room was completely closed off from the main barn with only an inside door. There was a small outside window through which the bushel baskets were passed and stacked. Dad spent many fall hours sorting and cleaning the potatoes for the peddle route. He had an small old radio that he listened to while he worked, often to Arthur Godfrey, a well known broadcaster and entertainer of the day.

When we became teenagers, both Bill and I declared that we were not interested in a farming career. Dad did not seem surprised and quickly looked towards other possible sources of income. Mom's younger brother, Uncle Chill, was having success in the service gas station business, so he encouraged Dad to move in that direction. He took training during 1950 and leased the Sunoco station in nearby Middletown. He did financially well in the gas station business, built his own location in Marietta during 1960 and remained there until he retired in the mid 1970's.

While he reflected it in many ways, Dad never expressed his love verbally. His eyes showed it through that pale blue twinkle especially at times when he was happy. One Christmas, my wife and I needed new tires for our car and affording them was not in the picture. We woke up to a snowstorm that morning and anticipated that Mom and Dad, who had planned to be with us, would not be traveling the some 75-mile snowy-road distance. However, about late morning, they arrived in their pickup truck and guess what was in the back of it? Yes, a new set of tires. Dad was laughing and so happy as Mom smiled warmly.

After being retired for some time, Dad and Mom visited us for one week in December 1982. It was a wonderful, happy time, which I will always remember. At the end of the stay, Dad was getting in the car preparing to drive home from North Carolina to New Mexico, where he now lived close to Bill and Marie. I hugged him and told him I loved him. He responded—for the first time ever—that he loved me too.

He and Mom had earlier retired in a small home in New Cumberland, Pennsylvania. However, after the Three Mile Island atomic power plant accident in March, 1979, they moved to New Mexico, near where Bill and his family lived.

There they grew beautiful flowers and many vegetables on a five acre plot where they also had a home constructed.

I truly felt that through irrigation and cultivation, a piece of New Mexico sand became a little oasis. Dad, still striving for perfection, and with the help of Mom, together reaped the rewards of hard work and dedication.

In May of 1988, Dad was diagnosed with esophageal cancer, another victim of the use of DDT insecticide. Like many other farmers, he was never warned of the potential danger in using this strong chemical. He died in December of that year.

The last time I saw Dad was late that fall in New Mexico when he asked me to take him for a ride in his pickup truck through the country. He told me where to turn and we drove all morning for many miles in areas I had never before seen. He was excited and especially upbeat.

I have the greatest respect for the positive way that he dealt with the ending of his life here on earth.

MOM

Caring, helpful, understanding. Mom was a worker in the fields, a sales person at the farmer's market, brought fresh produce to the front door on her peddle route, gave the utmost care to the baby chicks, and nurtured all of the farm animals. She also completed the daunting task of laundry every Monday. Mom was everything to her hard-driving husband. She was a supportive daughter-in-law and a wonderful, caring mother.

While Dad was a true workaholic and a farmer with the straightest rows of corn, he could never have made it without the support and love of Mom. She was always there for him and anyone else when needed. When our neighbors, the Cobles, had a family death Mom arose at 4:30 a.m. and went to their barn each morning for about five days and helped hand milk the some 35 cow dairy herd. How she had so much time to give each one of us, I will never know.

When we got sick, Dad was ready to put us back to work as soon as we improved. But Mom said, "No, the boys may not go out and do farm work, they need to get well first." I remember times Dad was so desperate for help that often a heated discussion ensued. Mom would not back down. She was as protective as a mother hen, her flock under wing. There were times that Mom said we were still sick so that we could rest another day. She had the ability to be manipulative and sometimes used that quality to get what she wanted. I worried that we were doing the wrong thing, as it was obvious that Mom was a bit devious.

Our neighbor across the road, Mrs. Strayer, lived alone. Her husband had passed away years earlier and her son was considered wayward. He lived elsewhere, but returned home for periods of time proving to be of no support. She had a live-in helper named Squire. No one knew his last name. He took care of her garden and small apple orchard, cut her firewood and did other chores, for which he received lodging. She prepared an evening meal for them both, but he seemed to be on his own for breakfast and lunch. Often hungry, Squire had a daily routine of coming by our kitchen very early in the morning. He was a friendly sort of fellow and Mom took a liking to him. Mom always prepared a cup of hot coffee when he entered our kitchen and directed him to the rocking chair by the stove. I do not recall Squire being invited to sit with the family for breakfast, but as soon as we were all off to the barn or field, she would give him a plate of leftovers, which proved quite substantial enough. Shortly thereafter, he ambled back down our long lane.

Monday was laundry day. No matter the weather, the clothing got washed on that day. Even in the coldest of winter, the sheets, overalls and towels got hung out on wire lines strung from wooden poles in the backyard. It was fascinating to touch a piece of laundry frozen solid and wonder just how they might dry. We had a wash machine that had a double roller for squeezing out excess water. Some things had to be washed by hand first and then put into the machine. It was often my job to turn all the socks inside out and rinse out the wheat chaff and other dirt. Large blue handkerchiefs which were used in the field and barn often needed hand washing in Clorox water. This was a disgusting job. Meanwhile Grandma Deimler would have a huge black iron kettle of water boiling over a wood fire near the summer kitchen in which she would put a bar of lye soap and "cook" the bib-overalls. She'd stir the pot as though she was making a beef stew and, when all the dirt was gone, she would rinse them by hand in a nearby tub filled with cold water and hang them out to dry. Laundry day has lots of memories because it was a team effort.

Mom did the same peddle route for many years in nearby Middletown. Tuesdays and Thursdays found her driving through neighborhood streets and stopping for customers along the way. The folks knew when to expect her and enjoyed the variety of fresh vegetables. With Saturday being Market day, Wednesdays and Fridays were wholesale days. The cash crops were tomatoes and peaches. With our large orchard, we sold a lot of peaches! Mom knew every store manager by name. With a smile and a little sweet talk, she always made a sale and often got them to buy even after they had said no. She sometimes ran late and Dad had a tendency to express his impatience that the job took more time than he expected.

I had some anxious times as an eleven-year-old youngster. A strange pain mysteriously developed in my right index finger. Many a night, I sat outside Mom and Dad's bedroom door crying quietly. Bill and I had just moved from the bedroom above the kitchen to the bedroom on the other side of the house next to Grandma's room. Even though Mom's door was always closed, she answered the call and came to comfort me.

The pain did not cease as we all hoped. We had a new physician, Dr. Rife Gingrich, MD, who was a general practitioner proficient in everything from delivering babies to surgery. The X-rays did not reveal a specific problem and so it was decided to cut open the finger for exploratory surgery. A small tumor on the bone which was pressing a nerve was found. Two small tumors from my right arm were also removed. The fear was that the laboratory report would reveal cancer, so there was great relief when the report came back as benign. My trip to Harrisburg General Hospital with a two-night stay was the furthest away from home I had ever been, a scary experience. But my finger healed, and the pain stopped. However, I have the scars to this day.

We had one or two cows for milk. Milking the cow was a twice-per-day necessity at 6 a.m. and again at 6 p.m. Mom and Bill did the milking most often. It was my least favorite job, mostly because my hands got so tired, but I frequently took a turn. Mom was certain that the intense hand exercise would help heal my finger, and it did seem good in regaining movement. The milk was consumed unpasteurized and kept cool in large earthen crocks in the refrigerator. Each day, the cream was skimmed and transferred to a separate crock for just cream. We kids did not like the taste or smell of raw milk, but that's what we had to drink. Using an old-fashioned shaker with a plunger on top, we poured a glass of milk, added one raw egg, a small amount of vanilla and a pinch of sugar. After some vigorous plunging, it almost tasted like a milkshake.

When a cow came into heat, she was walked to the Cobles farm for their bull to service. I was invited to help lead the cow about a mile down the road. All three children were given this opportunity at roughly age eleven. Mom used this time as an opportunity for sex education. I chuckle when I reflect on Mom's words, "Do you know why we are taking our cow to see the neighbor's bull, Tommy?" "Yes, mother" was my reply, because Bill had already briefed me on the subject. However, the story continued with Mom giving a complete description of the entire process, including the subsequent birth of a baby calf about nine and a half months later. Calves were fattened, but were not always butchered for our use. If cash was short, Dad sold the calf to a local butcher.

On Mom's birthday in April, Bill, Peggy and I hiked into the woods and found a dogwood tree in bloom. A bouquet of these beautiful flowers made a wonderful gift which Mom truly loved. Sometimes, we found honeysuckle and added their fragrance and beauty to the arrangement. The black locust tree bloomed a little later and usually were ready by Mother's Day.

Buying new clothing was rare, so it is an experience I recall vividly. Our favorite place to shop was the Hershey Department Store, an eight-mile drive from home. In early August, just before school began, we took an afternoon off to travel to Hershey. Usually Mom took us shopping, and we all relished this special time with her. It was fascinating to see the many floors of beautiful clothing. I was intrigued by the vacuum tubes used to send the cash payment to the business office. Never wearing blue jeans or bib-overalls to school, we usually got a new pair of slacks and a couple shirts and socks. New clothes were a pretty big deal as most often we wore hand-me-downs.

In the fall of 1951, Dad sold the farm, but the new owners would not move in until April of 1952, two months before my graduation from Hershey High School.

That last year on the farm was spectacular. Dad had gone to run the new gas station and Bill was studying electronics in New York City. That left twelve months of farming to Mom, Peggy and me. Bedridden from a stroke in March of 1951, Grandma Deimler passed December 25th, that same year.

Now was my opportunity to shine behind the wheel of the tractor. It was amazing how straight the furrows were, and it was a joy to survey the handiwork when the field was plowed. Mom was in charge, but I had lots of latitude to make plans and see that various projects were completed. Peggy now gathered the eggs and did much of the cooking while Mom and I completed the heavy work. We had fewer chickens and turkeys that year as we were clearly phasing out of the farm business. There was still much to be done, and days were as busy as ever. Dad helped when he had time, and my neighbor and best friend, Harry Shope, helped as well. I saw new resolve in my sister Peggy that year as she was an important part of our accomplishments.

Mom kept the books on our profits. We all worked very hard, and the rewards were numerous. After leaving the farm, She and Dad worked as a team many more years in the gas station and corner grocery business.

Mom's life journey continued with Dad as they eventually moved to New Mexico. She lived nearly eight years longer than him. She continued to grow her flowers, vegetables and even baked pies. She could be found frequently at the local farmer's market with her products for sale.

At that point in life, Mom longed to be with Dad. She passed away peacefully in August of 1995.

GRANDMA DEIMLER

No OTHER PERSON HAS HAD MORE INFLUENCE ON MY life than my Grandmother Deimler. Her character, her love and her deep faith have defined who I am today. Many of my long winter evening hours were spent in her living room at our house wrapped in a blanket, curled up on her sofa, talking or reading one of her books. It was just the two of us.

Her bookcase was an antique lawyer's case with hinged glass doors, and it was intriguing just to open it. The case and books belonged to her daughter Sarah. Old books, they all looked so interesting, and I read and browsed frequently.

Grandma always found a way to give me a mini lecture on what things in this world are right and what things are wrong. She was extremely religious and read her Bible regularly, believing and stressing that God was aware of our every action. We would be judged accordingly. She was opposed to the use of tobacco and alcohol and made no bones about telling me emphatically to avoid the sins associated with that kind of behavior.

What I have become today is not nearly as strict as Grandma would have preferred, but her teachings have molded me significantly. What she taught me about the reality of living a moderate life and remaining quite true to those matters, I consider a moral and Spiritual commitment.

While Grandma had a long list of farm duties, many of which involved cooking and serving meals, she found time for her first love: flowers. She had an old-fashioned rock garden displaying a variety of species. The garden extended beyond her porch door about thirty feet towards the field. In that particular field, long rows of peonies appeared to be an extension of her garden and produced beautiful blooms which were cut and sold in the farmer's market. With this backdrop, the beauty of her rock garden was even more stunning. I was her helper, planting new flowers and weeding the beds. From this experience, my love for flowers began.

Mom and Dad had a small section between the west side of our kitchen and the sidewalk just big enough to plant, and this became my own little flower garden. When fall arrived and with Grandma's help, I did cuttings which I put in tin cans I had painted with whatever was available in Dad's workshop. The many-colored cans adorned Mom's dining room windows where they received the afternoon sun. Geraniums and coleus were two of my specialties. They did not always look pretty as they struggled to take root. Sometimes water overflowed on the window sill, but Mom never complained. She had a good grip on what was really most important, and little did I know this passion would remain with me always.

Grandma had a busy life cooking, cleaning, checking the eggs and helping in numerous areas. One of the other specific jobs she had was hulling lima beans. Everyone wanted their lima beans out of the shell. I can still see Grandma with a metal basin in her lap filled with lima beans, sitting under the shade of a large ash tree in our backyard breaking them open one by one to remove the hulls, a tedious task.

Skimming cream and making butter was another of Grandma's jobs. When the cream crock was full, she would take it out of the refrigerator and sit it on the table. She never checked with a thermometer but always somehow knew exactly when it was the right temperature. The cream was then transferred to a butter churn, a large glass container about two or three gallons in size. The metal top had a set of wooden paddles attached with a gear mechanism and handle for turning. It was my job to crank the churn when Grandma gave me the go-ahead signal. I never tired of this task as it usually kept me from doing more strenuous work. It wasn't long until the cream became butter and grandma took over again. She worked the pale yellow butter with a wooden spoon, turning it over and over gently while periodically pouring the buttermilk into a glass jar which we all shared in drinking later.

Sunday afternoons were a pleasant time for all of us. It really focused on Grandma as many from her family came visiting. Often the house was overflowing with aunts, uncles and cousins. They primarily came to see Grandma, but of course we were included. While they did congregate in Grandma's quarters, they spent time with us as well, especially the cousins.

I remember how exciting it was when Gracie, Aunt Esther's daughter, came to the farm as she was a favorite of everyone. She was close to Bill's age, and they liked to hang out together leaving Peggy and me a bit jealous. Aunt Esther was Dad's sister. She and Dad were very close, and they came to the farm nearly every Sunday after church. Other cousins, Martha and Kay, came often, too.

In the summer of 1950, not long after I got my driver's license, I drove Grandma to Hyattsville, Maryland, a suburb of Washington, DC, to visit her daughter, Sarah, who lived there alone. We had only a few days, but I remember a fun driving tour of DC with Aunt Sarah at the wheel. While there, at Aunt Sarah's suggestion, I planned a trip back the following spring with my best friend Harry Shope to see the cherry blossoms. Harry and I went in March, 1951 and while there, we received a phone call that Grandma had had a stroke.

Unfortunately, the stroke was severe enough to cause her to become bedridden. I took care of her spring flower garden all summer and into the fall. Mom was her caregiver and did so without any outside help, while I assisted as much as possible. Many days I would cut a bouquet from her garden and bring it to her. I often sat with her quietly in the bedroom and shared what flowers were blooming. She could hear me, I am certain, but she could not respond.

Sadly, Grandma Deimler passed away on December 25, in 1951—Christmas Day. With the farm already sold, we would move during the coming April.

GRANDMA AND
GRANDPA MEINSLER

Mom's parents lived in a large, old two-story brick house with a huge kitchen about a mile south of Middletown. They had a family of six children, and Mom was the oldest. They were hard working and very poor, but their home was a very happy one.

Mom often told the following story from the 1930's, in the middle of the Great Depression. The family had so little, and no wood or coal with which to cook and keep the kitchen warm. There was a railroad along the border of their property, and the train cars filled with coal stopped close to their home regularly. She recalled her mother climbing to the top of a train coal car and throwing off large chunks of coal for their stove. Otherwise they would have had to experience living in extremely low temperatures. They did not think of this act as stealing, but one of survival.

Grandpa originally worked in the Baldwin Locomotive-Works known as the "steel foundry" near Steelton, Pennsylvania. He walked the three-mile trek each way daily as he never owned a car or learned to drive. Later on, when I was about six years old, he built a small convenience store and gas station on the edge of his property which provided their income until he retired many years later. His stop-and-go business was clearly a forerunner to the convenience stores of today.

Every Sunday evening our family piled into our pickup truck and headed to the Meinsler home. In the summer

Bill and I rode sitting on a bench placed against the cab in the truck bed. In the winter all five of us rode inside the truck cab. It was a one-seater, before the days of seat belts, so Mom usually held me while Bill held Peggy, with Dad driving.

Nearly every Meinsler family member was present on Sunday evenings, sometimes totaling twenty folks. Everyone crowded into the kitchen area about supper-time, crowded but cozy and fun. Having eaten only home-cooked meals on the farm, it was exciting to see the array of lunch meats, bread and potato chips. Of course, Grandpa grew vegetables including celery, tomatoes and lettuce, plus homemade foods like pickles, relish, pickled cantaloupe, red beet eggs, potato salad, and coleslaw. All these were displayed in home-style bowls placed around the table. Everyone brought something to add to the meal, ours most often being hard boiled eggs. The meal usually ended with homemade pie, cake or ice cream. I was in awe of this kind of cold lunch spread. We had never eaten potato chips, so Bill and I usually had seconds. They were in large tin cans that seemed to be bottomless.

While the spread was something to behold, especially for poor folks, the food itself was not what impressed me the most. In our home, the meals were generally a quieter time, just a bit serious. Here, the talking and laughter often got so loud and long that I almost felt nervous. Dad always set a serious tone at the table, but even he got into the spirit of Sunday evening at the Meinsler home.

Grandma and Grandpa sold milk, bread, soft drinks and potato chips, plus a huge assortment of candy and cakes at their convenience store. Their storage room for extra supplies was in a huge walk-in closet in their house, just off the dining room. Opening the door, the aroma of chocolate was overpowering. Grandma gave us a small brown paper bag and while opening the boxes for us to choose, threw in the first piece as a gift. We three kids always had about fifteen to twenty cents to spend. It is amazing how much chocolate we could buy for that small amount of money, and our bag was soon overflowing. Our favorites included the Klein's Grade A bar for one penny and the Mars Bar for two pennies.

As a supplementary source of income, Grandpa farmed his three acre property, growing an assortment of vegetables for canning and some to sell too. His largest crop was celery and I truly believe he had the best tasting celery in the area. He knew exactly how far apart to plant it, and he tilled the soil between the rows with a small single-engine gas cultivator. In the early fall before frost, he would board each side of the row of stalks using a heavy dark paper and stakes. This process bleached the celery prettier than I have ever seen it. Dad did not grow celery, so it was a treat to eat it there and often take some home.

There was a water spring at the corner of the yard which was lined with rock and had a locked door on it. They kept milk and often vegetables there. A large dipper hung on the wall, and it was fun to take a drink of the refreshing water. Along the one side was a rather large and hearty patch of watercress. It was used as a garnish on their table, but most of all we liked to take a large bunch home and eat a buttered bread watercress sandwich.

Many a Sunday afternoon when we were in our early teens, Bill, Harry Shope and I rode our bicycles to visit with them. We sat on one of their big rockers and munched on a bag of chips and had a soft drink from the ice-filled cooler. We listened to Grandpa complain about the increasing cost of gasoline as it rose from fifteen cents per gallon to eighteen cents. He expressed fear that the escalating price would put him out of business. But in 1952, before I went off to college, the cost was twenty cents per gallon, and his business was thriving, as was the automobile industry.

I always went by to visit when I was home from college and in the Army. After Shirley and I married and started a family, we too visited Grandma and Grandpa Meinsler. Shirley was once wearing a black sweater that I had given to her for Christmas, and when Grandma found out that I had given it to her, she lectured me by saying "you never give your sweetheart black clothing."

These were meaningful experiences as both grandparents were always so excited to see us. Departures were as much an occasion as the event itself. Everyone gathered in small groups outside on the lawn or sidewalk talking while my grandparents stood on the porch smiling and waving as the stragglers left.

Often times, Grandpa looked at Grandma and said, "Kate, just look at what you and I started."

BROTHER BILL

My brother, Bill, was born twenty-two months earlier than me on August 27, 1932. He was just a little bigger, but a lot stronger than me. In many ways, he was my hero. I always looked up to him, partly because he was older. With tradition on the farm, the oldest was expected to do the most and had larger responsibilities. It seemed to me that Bill had the more important jobs while I did the more mundane chores.

We were isolated on the farm and relied thusly on each other. So much work left little time for play. We got up early and did morning chores before school, walked a mile to and from the school house and considered each other to be best friends.

Bill was muscular and could carry a hundred pound bag of feed on each shoulder. He could lift just about anything. Not only could Bill carry heavier feed bags, drive the tractor better and get work done faster, but he also knew what needed to be done on the farm, when sometimes I did not. I believed he could do any thing and admired him for it.

Because he was the oldest and worked the hardest, I believe he and Dad had a special relationship. They often discussed what projects needed done the next day. Dad confided in him, and Bill was in the know in a lot of areas. Often, after lunch and during mealtime rest, Bill jumped on Dad and started a wrestling match. They rolled in the grass with boundless energy.

Farming wasn't Bill's passion. Early on in his life, he demonstrated his interest in electronics. His workshop was in the basement. He repaired the family radios, toasters and just about anything electric. He had headphones before they were popular and listened to the radio in bed each night. He built a speaker, attached it to a very long cord, and sat it near the barn so he could hear music or a talk show while working.

On the peak of our garage roof, he installed a huge antenna that he designed. The improved reception brought in radio stations from far away locations. Initially, Dad was upset because he feared the antenna would attract lightening. He calmed down once Bill explained how he had grounded the new device.

Dad and Mom relied heavily on Bill to make a difference in the day's endless list of chores. Bill never complained. Instead, he rolled up his sleeves and went to work. "Work hard, play hard" was his motto.

One of Bill's main jobs was to spray the vegetables and fruit trees for insects. The sprayer equipment consisted of a large tank that needed to be pulled by our tractor. The spray nozzle was operated manually, so the trigger was squeezed to start the spray. The tank held about a hundred gallons of water, and we mixed powdered DDT by hand, dipping in deep, usually past our elbows. When the pesticide DDT was first developed in the late 1940's, it was used heavily by farmers. Unfortunately, Dad, Bill and I all developed cancer from our use of DDT. Dad passed away from esophageal cancer, Bill is a prostate cancer survivor and I'm living with bladder cancer. After thoroughly mixing the DDT spray, Bill replaced the lid on the tank, and proceeded to spray the farm vegetables. Peggy and I shared the tractor driving duties, pulling the sprayer tank. Following numerous law suits, DDT was banned by the EPA in 1972.

In 1948, Dad and Mom bought their first passenger automobile, a brand new Pontiac. Bill was entering his junior year and I was beginning my freshman year at Hershey High School. As was the neighborhood plan, the older boys drove the family car while the younger siblings all rode along to the school. The Pontiac was a six passenger, four door vehicle, but most often we only had five people on board. The drive was about ten miles from our farm, and Bill drove most days, regardless of the weather.

After high school graduation, Bill attended RCA Institute in New York City where he studied electronics. It was a bold step for Bill to move that far from home and live in the shadow of the tallest city buildings. Dad and he made the long journey by car to Brooklyn and toured the campus and together they made the decision for Bill to attend the school. Off the harbor on a tiny spot of land named Big Brother Island in dormitory buildings is where Bill lived for most of the next two years. Being surrounded by water, Bill rode a ferry boat each morning and evening traveling to and from classes.

Taking a higher level course of math than he was prepared for, Bill found the coursework intense. It was a heavy dose of electrical engineering. Year-round studies provided Bill a math and physics equivalent to a bachelors degree.

Upon graduation, he went to work for Glenn L. Martin Aircraft in Baltimore where he was part of the team developing the Matador missile. The Martin MGM-1 Matador was the first operational surface-to-surface cruise missile built by the United States. It was similar in concept to the German V-1, but the Matador included a radio link that allowed in-flight course corrections.

Later, Bill transferred to their Florida location and continued both testing and development. While in Florida, he met and married Marie Walter, a sister of a work associate.

They raised four children and today have countless grand-children and great-grandchildren.

Bill went on to work for Ampex Recording which required a move to New Mexico. There he worked at White Sands Air Force Base. Bill joined a team of experts on their missile recording equipment used to track and transmit informational signals back to earth. His expertise in how this equipment functioned and the instructions on how to best operate it was of great value to Ampex. Bill's knowledge of the computer driven equipment was in much demand and he traveled worldwide to conduct workshops on the most efficient way to use it.

Bill and Marie are retired and continue to reside in New Mexico.

SISTER PEGGY

Peggy was born on January 22, 1937. Unlike her brothers, who were born in the farmhouse, she came into this world at Harrisburg General Hospital. For Dad, it was a little girl at last. Peggy was always a part of what happened on the farm, but her responsibilities were much different than mine. Most days I did not see her much. She was in the house helping Grandma.

With the kitchen serving such an important role, there was always much work to be done there. Bill and I referred to her as "Grandma's assistant" and she was exactly that. Grandma was in charge of the house and as such instructed Peggy on her chores as the day moved along.

Putting the dishes away was one of her regular jobs, and there were plenty to wash. Dishes were dried as soon as they were washed and immediately stored in the cupboard. Flies were a major problem and seemed to be everywhere, dishes included. The long sticky tape hanging from the ceiling was a deterrent, but many escaped that demise. Peggy and Grandma were a kitchen cleanup team and worked closely together to keep it spick and span.

Keeping the house clear of dirt and dust was a big challenge. Farmers worked in the ground outside all day long so it was difficult not to drag it into the house. Peggy used an old fashioned broom for sweeping, with a dustpan to catch the dirt.

Gathering the eggs was a morning and evening task. I did it much of the time, but Peggy was often called upon when we were busy with harvest or other projects. The full wire baskets were too heavy for her, and she sometimes spread out the load over a couple of baskets.

Peggy did not experience the strenuous activity of the barn and field. Even though Mom was out in the thick of it most of the time, Peggy, on the other hand, stayed housebound. However, her duties were still important in the grand scheme of farm operation. The one outside job for which Peggy was responsible was driving the tractor that pulled our insecticide sprayer for the peach orchard, other fruit trees and most vegetables. The equipment moved along slowly so that Bill could operate the hand spray nozzle. He would call for her to stop so that he could complete a certain tree or area, but with the engine noise of the tractor she sometimes did not hear him. She then received the full pressure of the spray on her back as a clearer signal. For some unknown reason, Peggy has fortunately escaped the dreaded cancer disease.

While it sometimes seemed to her brothers that Peggy got the easy jobs, her contributions were of vital importance. It was hard work for such a young girl. Grandma could not have done it alone.

In May 1949, Dauphin County closed the one-room schoolhouses. Peggy had just finished sixth grade. Families no longer had a choice of school systems, and all students then went to the Middletown Schools.

In high school, one of my fondest memories of Peggy was double-dating. She had a close friend, Janet, who was fun to be around. Bill dated her for a time, and when he went away to school, I began to date her. Peggy had a boyfriend in high school, and the four of us double-dated quite often. We talked and laughed a lot.

After seeing a movie, we would stop at a local drive-in restaurant for a hamburger, fries and coke.

My friendship with Peggy got even stronger during my years at Penn State University. We continued to socialize with friends when I came home on breaks. At college, I met and developed a close friendship with George Weimer. During my sophomore year, we became roommates. I began taking George home on weekends, and he soon struck up a relationship with Peggy.

Their wedding took place shortly before his graduation. George initially worked for the Pennsylvania State Forestry Service giving forest management support to woodland farmers. After a year or so, George and his parents purchased a dairy farm in Wisconsin, and the two families moved there. Life and the dairy business was challenging. They did not have farming experience to draw upon.

Peggy and George stayed on the dairy farm for twenty years before selling and moving to other opportunities. They raised five children while on the farm, and they too learned lessons from the land that have remained throughout their lives. Our families stayed in touch even as our busy, young married lives took us in varied directions.

Sadly, George passed away in February, 2010 quite suddenly with a brain aneurysm. Peggy initially remained in Wisconsin but has escaped the cold northern winters by moving to Florida where she will spend her remaining years enjoying the warm sunshine.

ONE-ROOM SCHOOLHOUSE

A S A SIX-YEAR-OLD FIRST GRADER, ATTENDING THE ONE-room Cobles School was a very scary moment. I looked up at the big brick building and knew this would be my daytime home for the foreseeable future. It was terrifying to walk up to the covered porch and enter the big heavy door. My little desk was to the far right corner next to the piano. With my head down my shy, somewhat small body stood up straight as we were asked to rise for the Pledge of Allegiance followed by the Lord's Prayer. We completed morning exercises with the singing of "My Country Tis Of Three." Our teacher, Miss Alice Demey, while playing the piano led us with much pride and formality.

Over time, the schoolhouse became a very cozy place to all of us, protected and safe from the outside world. A large furnace sat in the rear corner, next to a door in the floor which led to the coal and kindling storage. The older boys brought up the wood and coal to keep the furnace burning. We all took turns cleaning the building by sweeping the floors, which were a raw wood coated with a waxy, oily substance. Additional student jobs included washing the windows, dusting, chopping wood and fueling the furnace. Schoolhouse chores required cooperation and teamwork to get them done quickly, efficiently and with a good attitude.

Occupying the room were thirty wooden desks of assorted sizes, some small enough for a first grader and others large enough for an eighth grader. Winter coats and boots, much needed on cold winter days walking to and from school, were stored in a double closet on either side of the front door, girls in one location and boys in the other. We also put our lunch bag on the top shelf above our coats hanging on the hook. I always looked forward to Mom's bag lunches. She packed something good every day like bologna or turkey sandwiches and an apple or peach from our farm.

Outside the school house, we were surrounded by a field to the west, a hard surface road to the east, and school property to the north and south which served as our playground. An outside water pump with a well beneath was our only source of water. The pump was used often and in some ways provided fun. We raced to it and then took turns with the large iron handle.

All eight grades were Ms. Demey's responsibility. I learned to read with the story of "The Little Dog Who Lost His Bark." I heard the first graders start with that tale every year. Miss Demey stood behind her desk and announced, "First grade class, please rise, come froward." Each subsequent class, in turn, was asked to rise and move to the benches at the front of the room for their lesson. We then returned to our seats with a classroom assignment. Learning included a whole lot more than the basics of arithmetic or the art of penmanship.

First and foremost, students helped each other. If you had a talent for any particular subject, you edged along side of another's desk and shared your knowledge. My favorite was math and I became quite good at the basic concepts and passed that talent along quite willingly. I didn't know it back then, but teaching a fellow pupil was the best way to reinforce your own knowledge.

Discipline was never a problem. All students were well behaved. The children were polite and listened to teacher instructions closely. One item was a key factor in maintaining a stable environment. Just behind the teacher's desk and laying on the top edge, a wooden paddle roughly three inches in width and three feet long hung above the chalk board at the front of the room. The fact that it was there was a deterrent alone. I do not recall it being used, except for one time when a boy was causing trouble. In this situation, Miss Demey sent all the students outside, locked the door and closed the window shutters on the front porch. Not one of us ever knew what happened inside. The student did not appear to be distraught, but the school was very quiet for the next few days.

In sixth grade, we got an assignment to select a book from the school library, a shelf of well known books. Each student was required to stand in front of the class and give an oral book report. This was a most formidable task during my early education. I was scared to death of standing before my fellow students. One book I shall always remember was titled, *Scarface, The Story of a Grizzly*. The narrative tracks the life of a grizzly bear from birth and showed the challenges and dangers he faced in his struggle for survival. The book seemed very real to me.

We had to purchase only one book, *101 Famous Poems*. It was a variety of the best with poets such as Elizabeth Barrett Browning, Emily Dickinson, Robert Frost, Henry Wadsworth Longfellow and Edgar Allen Poe. It was a requirement to memorize many of the writings and recite them for the class. My favorite poem, part of which I can still recite, is "A Psalm of Life" by Longfellow. Both books can be purchased these many years later.

Each year, we celebrated Halloween with a variety of games. Our favorite was bobbing for apples, which gave everyone a chance to join in the fun. Our very strict teacher relaxed a bit that day, and the wet clothes and water on the floor were all part of the fun. One particular year, in the middle of our celebration, there was a loud bang on the door. Miss Demey answered the knock to greet someone dressed as a a witch wearing a long black gown, a black bonnet and dark mask. A large broom became the focus of our attention as pretend cob webs were swept from the walls and ceiling. A great mystery surrounded the visit, and after much maneuvering, the scary witch exited the door, never to be seen again. It was many years later that I found out the witch was really my mother. She must have laughed all the way back to the farm.

Winters in Pennsylvania were severe with snowfall of a foot or more during the night. In the mind of our teacher, there was no excuse for being absent because of snowfall. Snow or not, school was open every single day. Mom and Dad kept us home on one particular day after an all night snow storm that continued throughout the next day. The following morning the Deimler children were reprimanded in front of everyone. We never missed another day because of snow!

Although the furnace was allowed to die out on Friday evening, the students found it toasty warm on Monday mornings. When winter arrived, one of the older boys was selected to help build the furnace fire for the coming week. When I reached the seventh grade, I was chosen for what all the others considered a special honor. Each Sunday afternoon about 1:30, Miss Demey picked me up at the end of our long farm entrance lane. From there, she took me to school to assist in build the furnace fire for Monday morning. Just the two of us worked together to get the job done. I climbed the steep steps to the room underneath the school and first filled the bucket with kindling wood to start the fire. Miss Demey reached down as I handed the bucket up to her. After a roaring wood fire, the coal was added. We stayed there long enough to have red hot coals and then banked the draft to hold it over the night. I had this responsibility for two years and at the end of the year, I received a personal gift for my hard work: first a necktie and then a wallet.

Our favorite snow game was called "windmill." We lined up the entire school with the older children out front. Trudging through the snow, this long line of students formed a big windmill shaped track. Then we put in the spokes with a large hub in the center which became home base. The diameter of the windmill was maybe 100 feet. Then the game became one of tag. Someone was declared "it" and the fun began. You had to stay inside the track or you were immediately "it" and, of course, the idea was to tag another person. The only truly safe place was the large hub in the center, home base, where we sometimes piled quite high.

Periodically, the Public Health Nurse dropped in unannounced. She checked for personal hygiene, our overall health appearance and communicable diseases. Sometimes she checked our teeth, but mostly she just looked us over quite thoroughly. One year a student got scarlet fever. This was very contagious, so all of his books were removed from his desk and burned behind the school. I walked past his farm house and saw the large quarantine sign on the front door. He did not return to school for four weeks.

In the spring, just before school closed for the summer, we planned a picnic. Bill, Peggy and I brought a little wagon to load with goodies, including a jug of homemade lemonade. Everyone came with something special to eat and share with others. The outing involved a hike into the countryside. We played games and ate our special lunch. It was a highlight and helped end the year with the best of feelings.

I attended this rural school for eight years. It provided the farm boys and girls of our community with an education from first through eighth grade. Most of my fellow classmates completed their education with their graduation and went on with the business of farming. My dad, however, realized the importance of a good education and planned for us to continue to high school and even college.

Upon completion of the eight grade, a county examination was required for entrance into high school. By the time I reached eighth grade, many students had come and gone, and only Betty and myself remained to take the exam. Eight others in the county from three other one-room schools joined us. When the results were in, Miss Demey proudly announced that Betty's score ranked number one and I was number two in the county!

In September of 1940, the year I started first grade, Miss Demey was about twenty-four and beginning her fourth year of teaching. For thirteen years, until 1950, she was the teacher in that one-room school. She went on to teach in the Middleton schools after the one-room schoolhouse era came to an end. She retired with over fifty years of service. She was such an amazing teacher they named a school after her.

SNOW AND COLD

THE SNOW CAME AND THE WINTERS WERE COLD. IT WAS quite common in Pennsylvania to have snow on the ground throughout most of the winter months. We kids were excited when the flakes started to fall with it beginning many times in the early evening. How beautiful it was, a blanket of white covering the landscape for as far as one could see. It was smooth and untouched like the icing on a freshly baked cake. Only the footprints of our cats and dogs broke the even surface. The world seemed calm and quiet, giving one a feeling of serenity.

The depth often reached a foot or more by morning and the work started as the sky began to clear and daylight appeared. Shoveling snow was everyone's job with long trenches to the many buildings. The layout of trails seemed to provide a map of our farm with buildings scattered about in a roughly designed master plan.

The first priority was a wide path to the barn's lower level quarters where the animals were housed. Smaller side runs were dug to the upper part of the barn where the hay and straw were stored. Next, we needed a path to all the chicken and turkey pens. Then a route to the toilet, woodshed and workshop completing the snow shoveling.

Dad usually got up early on these mornings and the project was well under way when we awoke. I think he realized how difficult a job this was and wanted to spare us from part of that work. Dad was like that, but he never gave us the impression we were not responsible for a fair amount of what had to be done.

Winter had it's many challenges as we struggled to win against the elements of the sub zero temperatures which arrived along with the ice and snow. The long stretches of galvanized water pipes, most of which were buried underground, sometimes froze and even broke as the freezing water inside fought for space to expand. These pipe lines provided water to the poultry pens, some as far as 100 yards away from the main buildings. Sometimes they froze just where they came out of the ground and a blow torch was necessary to thaw them. In the meantime, pails filled with water had to be carried to the various buildings. This was very difficult and the heavy buckets often splashed water on my legs, a most uncomfortable feeling of wet and cold.

After clearing the walkways we still had to do the morning chores, and time was fleeting. Soon we would be heading off to school. We did the work quickly and gathered in the warm kitchen for a hearty breakfast that Mom had prepared. With head down, looking at my cold, red fingers, not wanting to appear weak, I exclaimed, "my fingers are so cold." With a hug, Mom lifted me even closer to the stove and I was comforted by her strong arms and much warmer temperature. My hands showed the results of intense farm labor as a row of thick calluses crossed my palm and another layer on the mid section of my fingers were hard and swollen.

The long lane from our house to the main road, Rural Route 441, was about 300 feet long and now needed to be opened. We used the tractor to make wheel tracks for our pickup truck. As we looked up the highway on one particular morning, we could see the snow was too deep for our truck. About that time, along came our teacher with her car being led by the big model Farm-All tractor driven by one of her brothers.

Dad's decision to use our tractor and wagon for the school run was the right one. We made good time through the drifts and picked up neighbor kids as we traveled. Much laughter and fun along the way made the trip to school quite an exciting experience.

With snow still clinging to our boots, soon the warmth of the big stove in the school house corner became the gathering point for some twenty students. Everyone was expected to be there regardless of the snowstorm and even with roads still covered. Miss Demey called the group to order at precisely 8:00 a.m. As if we did not have enough of that white precipitation already, when recess arrived at mid-morning, we took to the playground and began our usual snow games!

HOMEMADE DRINKS IN THE SUMMER

Along about June, it was beginning to get quite hot in Pennsylvania. The workers in the field were enjoying large jugs of water and sometimes a treat of something special.

There was not a large number of different drinks available but cold water was most plentiful. Farmers had to be careful not to become dehydrated so fluid intake was important. We longed for something different, however commercial soft drinks were not an item we were able to afford. Occasionally we were surprised with a kettle of fresh lemonade.

Lemonade was Mom's own recipe using real lemons. A large earthen gallon crock was used, slicing about six to eight lemons into it. Then sugar was added followed by a vigorous stomping with a hand potato masher. This process left a thick syrupy mixture of lemons, juice and sugar. The crock with mix, filled with water and ice, provided a full gallon of the best lemonade one could find anywhere. It was easy to make and considered a real treat by the workers and we kids as well.

Root beer was the real hot weather treat. Mom tried, but could not keep the summer tradition of making root beer a surprise. My guess is that she waited for a rainy day when outside work slowed down to take the necessary time to make it.

The various bottles emptied of catsup not long before began to appear in the summer kitchen. They would not be needed for catsup until September when again they would be filled with this unique home made condiment.

Upon seeing the empty bottles, I smiled to myself and knew we would soon be drinking home made root beer. I cannot recall the exact recipe, but know for sure the ingredients stirred into the water included sugar, root beer extract and yeast. She carefully poured the mixture into the sparkling bottles and capped them in the same precise way she always did.

Next the beverage needed to age. The bottles were placed on their side in one of our large galvanized laundry and all purpose tubs. Layer upon layer of bottles filled the tub nearly to the top. Waiting was the tough part. While the aging time was a matter of only two weeks, it seemed like forever.

The tubs were carefully moved to the corner of the summer kitchen where they would be out of the way. This area was always a beehive of activity so everything had to be in it's assigned space.

At least once a day, and often more times, I would peep into the tub to check the bottles. I could see the bubbles moving, indicating fermentation was taking place. It looked so appealing, and I knew now it would not be long.

At last, the word came that the root beer was ready. Oh the taste—I never drank anything so refreshing, it was so good. Some of it was placed into the refrigerator to cool for later drinking. Everyone got the chance to open their own bottle. Soon the supply became depleted, as we thirsty ones consumed it rapidly. But before summer passed by, at least one more batch of root beer was made and enjoyed.

WORLD WAR II

I WAS SEVEN YEARS OLD ON DECEMBER 7, 1941. LIKE MOST folks, we heard it on the radio that Sunday morning. I did not understand the full impact of a Japanese attack on Pearl Harbor, but stress on the faces of my parents was very clear. In the weeks ahead, I realized that our country was at war.

My heart pounded at the thought of Dad going off to fight in the military. I knew that would be very dangerous and perhaps he would be wounded or not even return home. Thankfully, we soon learned that a man with three children, age 32 and farming full time, would not be drafted.

Dad went to work at nearby Middletown Air Force Base, a major parts supply center for airplane repair and assembly. Another function of the base was to train young pilots learning to maneuver their plane to attack the enemy. I commonly witnessed these single engine planes going into a steep dive directly above our farm land.

I was both proud and pleased that Dad worked there during the war. I felt the importance of his role in the world-wide conflict. However, life on the farm was even busier for those years. Again, our entire family worked together to keep the farm operating.

Everyone throughout the country became involved in the "war effort." Nearly all foods and many natural resource were rationed. We were issued ration books with little coupons to submit when making a purchase. Meat, sugar, lard and gasoline were among the most scarce. Farmers were allocated more of things like sugar and gasoline because of their critical impact on the world food supply. Members of the family felt the pain of not having enough, but Dad and Mom always found a way to share any extra food or gasoline from our supplies. The war effort was about helping and sharing.

The idea of recycling actually began in the 1940's when the nation was engulfed in World War II. Folks even tried to out do each other. Slogans like, "Don't waste anything" and "save what you don't use" became an emphasis for everyone. If you didn't use it or if you could do without, it was saved. There were huge drives for unused iron and all forms of metal. We started a scrap pile behind the barn with things like worn out plow shears, old tin cans and other forms of metal which were then picked up by war volunteers monthly. It was encouraging to see the pile grow and know it would help provide equipment and ammunition to our soldiers.

Simple things like saving extra fat from frying bacon and pouring it into a can for making glycerin and explosives became a near obsession. We had many products on the farm that others had difficulty obtaining. Sugar and flour were hard to find as they were mainstays. Sugar was a must for canning, which in the world of farming was a necessity. Dad carried a 100-pound bag of sugar on his shoulder into the shed and Mom knew she could begin to can food that was overripe and still on the vine.

Dad required that we eat every scrap of food on our plate before leaving the table. My brother took too many mashed potatoes one evening and he sat for an hour before he could eat the rest. He was then be allowed to go to a 4-H meeting.

The school often had a war drive of it's own and we took some of the things we saved, like scrap iron. Even the foil on chewing gum was important. Our collective efforts were amazing.

I collected milkweed pods and Bill helped also. These mostly wild plants grew in wet farmlands that were not normally cultivated. The pod was about five inches long and contained seeds that had silky floss-like fuzz with waterproof qualities. The Japanese occupation of Java in the Dutch East Indies cut off US supplies of kapok, used in pilot's life vests, so the milkweed provided a substitute. We gathered the pods in the fall of the year as they ripened. We then bagged them in large burlap or mesh bags so that the air could flow through and dry them. It took two large bags to manufacture one life vest, and we later learned that this project across the US provided over a million life vests for our Navy and Air Force.

My uncle, Chill, spent the war years in the Navy in the South Pacific as a gunner on the destroyer USS Borie. I pictured him wearing a life vest made from milkweed fuzz. I felt like I was helping fight the battles and win the war.

We wrote letters and sent comic books to our relatives who were fighting in the war, cousins Bobby Deimler, Sock Deimler and Don Gallagher. Mail was important to all the GI's and mail call was one of the highlights of the day.

Victory finally came in 1945 when I was eleven years old, and the nation went back to business as usual.

FAMILY VISITS

Aunt Esther, Uncle Bill and their daughter, Grayce, often visited us on the farm on Sunday afternoon, a true highlight. Aunt Esther was faithful in coming to see us, especially her own mother. As Dad's oldest sister, she took a special liking to him and her affection was quite obvious. To me, Aunt Esther was a supporting, caring and loving person. She seemed at peace with the world, her family and her God. Later on, whenever my family and I visited her, she always served lunch and made us feel so welcome.

Aunt Esther's husband, Bill Gallagher, always came along to see us. He was a relaxed person, as though he never had a care in the world. I usually helped him pick up over ripe peaches that had fallen to the ground and carried the basket for him. He had some respiratory issues, and he struggled to breathe.

Uncle Bill and I both shared an interest in baseball. During high school, I began to follow the Cleveland Indians, which became my favorite team. Uncle Bill always had a radio to his ear listening to games intently. He and I often talked about who would win the pennant and play in the World Series. Uncle Bill loved to eat roasted turkey on the farm. He asked for the turkey carcass after the meal and picked it apart, piece by piece, savoring every morsel. When he was done, nothing but a pile of bones remained.

Grayce's three brothers usually did not come along because they were older teens and had other interests. Jim, Don and Dick were only there on very rare and special occasions.

Other members of Dad's family came by on Sunday afternoons as well. They were mostly there to see Grandma. Grandma's quarters were large enough for lots of company, but the crowd overflowed to our side of the house numerous times.

Dad's other sisters were Marion and Sarah. Aunt Sarah was a single divorcee who was very much a career person. She was the executive secretary for the president of a ship building company in Tampa. She dressed in the finest clothes and gave the air of self confidence. Her manner was outspoken with strong convictions. She later moved to Hyattsville, Maryland. I visited her there several times.

Aunt Marion was the most outgoing with a happy demeanor, laughing often. After an unhappy initial marriage, she owned a boarding house in Middletown. There she met and later married John Lund. When I was in high school, Uncle John invited Bill and me to visit them where they lived in West Grove, Pennsylvania. We traveled there by train and had a wonderful time fishing on a nearby lake.

Uncle Rob and my Dad did not associate very much, perhaps because Rob was given the first chance to run the farm, but did not. He and his wife had two sons and a daughter. Cousins Bobby and Sock sometimes dropped by, and I got to know them. Bobby was a marine and fought at Iwo Jima in the war. Sock was a machine gunner and fought in Europe. I never knew their daughter Lottie very well.

Dad's brother Walter came on special holidays. Dressed in a suit, he projected feelings of importance. He always had something special for Bill, Peggy and me in his pocket. I still have the pair of magnetic dogs he gave me long ago, on one of those visits. He and his wife Jean had two daughters, Martha and Kay. They visited on Sundays as well, and because they were so upbeat, their presence helped make it a fun time.

Of all the Sunday company, the presence of cousin Grayce was felt the most. Grayce was a fun-loving, highly spirited young person. My siblings and I competed for her time when she came. However, she and Bill, being of the same age, had much in common and spent the most time together. Grayce could make Dad laugh more than anyone else. By that time, Dad was completely bald, and she always found a way to kiss him on his bald head. Laughter always erupted at this moment.

Mom's family rarely came to the farm. Aunt Dot and Uncle Chill visited once in a while, mostly they came to help out with farm work. Occasionally, Aunt Lill and Uncle Paul spent time with us in addition to their part-time work there.

The Pennsylvania Turnpike was big news around 1950. The route of this road was about a mile from our farm and cut through the back corner of the Coble's dairy farm. Everyone was fascinated by this new limited access highway with two lanes going each way. While the first sections opened nearly a decade before, the final portion was finally being completed. Harry and I would slide down the bank with our bicycles to access the turnpike and then ride for miles on the concrete highway before it opened to the public. On several occasions after it opened, Uncle Paul, Aunt Lill, Mom, Dad, Peggy and I got a Sunday turnpike ride as far as Pittsburg in Uncle Paul's new six passenger Pontiac.

Both Uncle Chill and Uncle Paul enjoyed fishing. Uncle Chill liked to fish for shad at Conowingo, a hydro-electric dam in the Susquehanna River just across the state line in Maryland. Spring was the best time of the year, and Bill and I were occasionally invited to go with him. Early, even before daylight, the shad might be active. If so, we came home with an outstanding catch.

Dad, early years on farm; Dad, Tom, Peggy and Bill; Dad, plowing
with mules Kate and Rose

Mom, early years on the farm; Mom, dressed as witch at one room school; Mom, Tom, Peggy and Bill

Bill, Peggy and Tom; Bill and Tom, dressed for Sunday School;
Bill, Peggy and Tom, raking the field

Bill, Peggy and Tom in the back yard; Tom and Bill, front
porch; Tom and Bill, having gathered the eggs

Grandma Deimler and Peggy in back yard; Grandma Deimler, Bill, Peggy and Tom in backyard; Grandpa Deimler in chicken yard; Grandpa Meinsler, Grandma Meinsler and Yvonne, Buddy (Bill's first two children)

Bill, Bubbles (dog) in side yard; Tom, Mike (dog) and Bill in front
yard; Mom and Mike (dog) in back yard; Old Workshop

Uncle Paul was more interested in the Delaware Bay where deep sea fishing was popular. A day trip there was quite exciting during our high school years. We had our own rods and reels, and we took along lard cans for icing down the fish. Typically Uncle Paul rented a small boat for a private outing. Off into the bay we sailed. The waters were usually calm, but on one particular occasion, a "Nor'easter" came up quickly. We found ourselves in the middle of a severe storm. Waves higher than our boat crashed down upon us as we clung to the sides for our lives, the winds tossing our little craft around like a cork in the pond. I was not fully aware of the imminent danger, but Uncle Paul was concerned that we may not make it home. The captain held the wheel steady, and in time the waters smoothed out. It really didn't matter that the fish were not biting on that day.

The contractor business was booming and Uncle Paul and Aunt Lill did extremely well during the early 1950's. They leased an acre or two on a small island in The Susquehanna, just north of Three Mile Island. There, they built a summer cottage, a picnic shelter and a little cabin with bedrooms for guests. The complex included a boat and swimming dock along the river. Having learned to swim in high school, I felt at ease with the many water activities. I became competent on water skis and enjoyed the high speeds, quick turns and maneuvering of Uncle Paul's inboard fifteen foot boat. They invited me to visit quite often on weekends, and I always had a fun time with my three male cousins, all just a bit younger than me.

CHRISTMAS

CHRISTMAS WAS BUSY AND HECTIC FOR THE DEIMLER'S. Slaughtering, cleaning and delivering turkeys consumed us all. We often finished the last of the turkey-cleaning in the late afternoon on Christmas Eve. Mom delivered that last turkey to the customer's homes before the day was over, ready to be cooked for Christmas dinner.

In the evening, after the barn-work was done, I went to the Grant Auch Christmas tree farm, just over the hill at the back of our land, and cut a tree for our family. We got advance permission from Grant, so he knew we'd be cutting our tree on Christmas Eve.

Mom and Dad had a long relationship with Mr. Auch He was a friendly, laid back sort of fellow who always took time to talk with Bill and me. His daughter, now my Aunt Dot, was courted and married by Mom's younger brother Charles. There was more of a connection than just being neighbors.

I often saw Mr. Auch when hunting season was in full swing, and found him in the hay field next to the Christmas trees. He carried an old double-barreled shotgun, the kind with hammer firing pins. The pins were always pulled back, and he was ready to shoot if prey came into view. The readiness of his gun caused me to be nervous. He was always in the mood to talk when he saw us, which I enjoyed. He was at least sixty-something and I was just a teen-ager, so our conversation made me feel important.

Dad and Mr. Auch had a farm-for-the-half mutual agreement. I believe it was strictly verbal, mainly because I never heard otherwise. He seemed like that kind of person. Mostly, we planted corn, wheat and hay in crop rotation. Some of his land was too steep to farm, so on these acres is where he planted evergreen trees for sale at Christmas, providing yet another source of income.

In total, we farmed about forty acres of his land, which gave us the opportunity to plant more than one crop. As was the custom, farming land belonging to another person, the owner provided the land, seed and fertilizer while Dad did the planting, cultivating and harvesting. Each person then received one half of the crop harvested.

Mr. Auch's trees were not precisely pruned shapes. Instead, they had curves and crooks here and there. Imperfect, the same as all of us. I looked them over until we found one to my liking. They were already well picked over from his sales by Christmas Eve, so that it was difficult to locate a truly good one.

Once we got the tree back home, we set it up in the living room. This room was not used often. Even so, it had a worn look to it, though it was saved for more formal use. The furniture was old wicker with a few broken fibers throughout. The rug was well worn, and not the best looking. An old floor lamp was on a small table in the corner.

We unpacked the tree decorations, including a grand array of old bulbs and colors that had been stored all year in the third floor attic. The electric lights had their own challenge because if one bulb was burned out the whole string went dark. We often spent considerable time exchanging bulbs to try and find the one which was out.

Finally, we'd get the lights working and all the decorations in place. It was satisfying to sit back and view our handiwork; the tree looked so great in spite of it being crooked and without an abundance of decorations. On

Christmas morning, our tree seemed taller and more beautiful than the night before.

We all gathered around the Christmas tree in the morning and opened our presents. Even though Grandma had her own quarters, she joined in for this special occasion. It was a happy time for all of us. We now could rest, laugh and be thankful for a good year.

As Dad did not often express his love for us openly, I realize now more than ever that he made little gestures to show how much he loved his family. As tired as he was, Dad annually played Santa Clause. On several years we found Santa asleep on our sofa. Oh, how exciting that was! Following gifts of oranges, Santa, with a ho-ho-ho, trudged off into the snow and early morning light.

SUNDAY FUN-DAYS

We squeezed tons of activity into Sundays, which Dad, except for the ritual of planning for the next week, considered a day of rest. While the cows, pigs, mules, chickens and turkeys had to be cared for seven days a week, we made expert use of our spare time. A typical Sunday fun-day might include church, a bike ride to the grandparents', climbing the big ash tree near the house, basketball by the barn, shooting bottles with our rifles at the farm dump or a hike in the woods. But, sometimes it also included an adventurous activity as described in the following accountings.

In the eyes of Dad, the annual Farm Show in Harrisburg was an event not to be missed. He made certain we got to it. All of the best farming equipment, newest farming methods and blue ribbon animals were displayed there. It was held in January, so the winter work load allowed us to spend a weekend afternoon enjoying the ambience of this unique show, truly a farmer's delight.

Hunting season also provided an opportunity for a change of pace. Dad taught us gun safety and how to hunt and shoot rabbits and pheasants. Thanksgiving Day morning was reserved for a hunting party with neighbors. This endeavor provided additional food for the table and a change of diet. Bill was the best shot and often brought home more than anyone else.

On very rare occasions, Dad would take us fishing on a Sunday afternoon. His favorite place to fish was Swatara Creek, a tributary of the Susquehanna River, on the east side of Middletown. Except for the typical sunfish, I did not catch many fish, but always enjoyed the outing.

Our extended family gathered for a Sunday picnic at Hershey Park at least once a year. In those days, the park was free and open to the public. It was beautiful with lots of picnic tables, ponds with ducks and gorgeous flowers. The rides were nearby, and you could purchase tickets for five cents at various ticket booths scattered throughout. Rides were no more than one or two tickets. One could have a truly fun afternoon for not much more than one dollar.

Our neighbor, Mrs. Strayer, had an apple orchard that was very old, receiving little care and deteriorating rapidly. Every fall it produced a minimal harvest, but we always got a few apples to eat. After the first frost, her handyman, Squire, gathered the dropped apples and made cider with a hand press. She was very generous with the cider as we always had a few jugs to enjoy!!

Mother's Day was another special holiday. The wild locust trees were in full bloom. Bill and I hiked into the woods, sometimes climbing up the locust tree to cut a bouquet of the aromatic flowers and bring them home as a gift for Mom. On several occasions, we went out to eat dinner at Aunt Sally's Kitchen in Elizabethtown. The lines were always long, but it was the only time we ate at a restaurant. It was a special treat. Little did I know that Shirley and her sister BJ both worked there as waitresses during that same period of time.

Birthday's were also a fun time. I loved fresh peach homemade ice cream, and it topped the list. Sometimes, we still had a few strawberries on June 29th, which I enjoyed. Peggy's birthday in January was more likely to get vanilla ice cream. There was usually a cake made by Grandma or Mom, candles and all. We often invited Harry Shope and Junie Harbold and Junie's mother Mabel (Mom's best friend), all close neighbors. They were not expected to bring gifts, and I usually got something special from Mom and Dad like a knife or ammo for my rifle. It was a custom for all the farm boys to take their driver's license test on the day of their sixteenth birthday. That day in 1950 was a very happy moment in my life, as I passed the test easily.

Dad took us to a barber shop in town which we considered a great opportunity to get away from the farm toils. There was just one barber who was always quite busy. The cost for a haircut was thirty five cents. Appointments were never taken. About fifteen chairs were arranged in a circle around the room, filled with waiting customers, and we just kept track of our turn. On a table in the center of the room was a huge pile of outdated magazines, including my favorite comic books, *Dick Tracy*, *Batman* and *The Lone Ranger*. This provided ample entertainment while we waited. The barbering style of the 1940's was "clippers to the side" leaving hair extremely short along the sides, but longer on top.

I liked to make trips to Mrs. Strayer's dilapidated barn. The structure was deteriorated badly and was quite unsafe. We were not supposed to go there but found it too intriguing to stay away. One morning, I heard the soft meow of baby kittens beneath some fallen beams, but out of sight. I could tell where they were located and so followed the sounds as I crawled through the maze of fallen wood.

In the shadows of a poorly lighted corner, I came upon a mother cat with a litter of kittens. Reaching into the wiggling little ones, I caught the cutest little ball of gray fur. Carrying it home carefully, I found Mom working nearby. "Mom, may I keep him?" I asked. "Yes, of course you may," she answered. She probably wondered why, with all the farm cats around, I wanted another one. And so, Sam cat became a part of our close family and lived many years, moving with us from the farm to our new home along the Susquehanna River.

Getting hay from the high loft in the barn to the floor below where the animals lived was more than just a job. While we were up there, we enjoyed jumping at least twenty feet from the cross beams into the deep hay. With a pitch-fork, we put the hay down the chute to the animal quarters underneath. Then we switched to the other side of the barn and did it all over again with the wheat straw, bedding for the cows and mules.

Oh how much we wanted a basketball net, but there was nowhere to put it. So we improvised and decided to attach the net to the east side of the barn. It was not the greatest spot because the playing area was a hard, stone driveway. But a couple of shots on the way to milk the cow, if only for a few minutes, was also a pleasant interlude. Mostly on Sunday afternoons, we played for an hour or so.

HARVEST TIME

FARMING IS THE BUSINESS OF PRODUCING A HARVEST. THE process of gathering mature crops from the fields is the culmination of planting, cultivating and nurturing which took place during the previous months. The results are in direct proportion to the care given, the weather during the growing season and the timing of the harvest itself.

For a truck farmer like us, the harvest is continuous, beginning with asparagus in the spring through potatoes and turnips in the fall. Asparagus grows quickly with cutting necessary morning and evening. I went with my wicker basket and paring knife, and cut the slender shoots just under the soil. Potatoes came late in the year, just about the time of early frost. On a chilly fall morning, we dug and stored away the potatoes in the barn for winter sale.

The first big field crop of the new year was hay which came in mid-June. This was saved and put in the barn for feeding our animals and was not a for-sale product. Following recommended crop rotation, Dad had sowed alfalfa and timothy seed along with the wheat during the fall of the previous year. These seeds all sprout in the fall and develop a strong root system, then when the wheat is cut the next summer, the hay is well established and growing nicely. These young well developed grass plants grow rapidly and soon will become a productive hay cutting.

In the early years, our hay was brought into the barn on mule drawn wagons. Loose hay was loaded by pitchfork with one worker on top of the wagon distributing the hay evenly. I often found myself spreading the hay on the top of the wagon. The hay was thrown up rapidly with the person on the wagon sometimes getting covered. The hay was next unloaded into the barn using a two pronged release fork that could lift a huge amount of hay by rope and pulley at one time.

Later on, when I was about ten years old, we had our hay bailed, and I drove the tractor pulling the wagon. I could barely reach the clutch and brake petals. Dad and Bill were throwing the hay bales onto the wagon where Mom was stacking them. We came to a slight hilly grade, and I could not put enough pressure on the pedals to stop. Down the hill we went, tractor and hay wagon out of control. Dad ran to my rescue, and stepping between the large rear wheel and the controls, stopped the tractor with his hands on the clutch and brake. I was very scared, afraid I did something wrong. It left me with a haunting memory.

We harvested wheat in July, which we cut with equipment that tied each bundle with binder's twine. The sheaths shuttled up a canvas platform and were kicked out the side of the machine into the field. We followed just behind, picking up each bundle of straw loaded with ripe grain at the tip and arranging them in the wheat shock. These large shocks were left in the field for about one week giving them a chance to dry and ripen more. We hoped that it would not rain during that time so that the threshing machine could do it's job and separate the grain from the straw. If the shocks became wet and stayed that way, the grain would sprout and spoil while still in the field.

Neighboring farmers who had the equipment did the threshing for a fee or for a share of the grain. We scheduled a day and again hoped for sunshine. The machine was large, about twenty feet long, twelve feet wide and fifteen feet high. On the top, a long tube about fourteen inches in diameter blew out the straw. The wheat grain came out below, now completely separated, and as it came out the chute it was bagged in burlap. At the end of the long pipe on top of the thresher was a blower hood through which the straw, chaff and dust passed at considerable force. This blower hood needed to be hand-guided so that the straw would be distributed evenly in the barn. The pipe was passed through the side of the barn and rested on the highest large cross beam in the peak of the barn roof.

I was not given a choice, but simply told to climb up the ladder which was part of the interior barn structure. From the top, I maneuvered my way to the large cross beam that ran along the outside wall. It was a very scary thing for a young man about twelve years old to have to do. The blower pipe was entered though an opening from the outside and my job on wheat harvest day was to position myself next to the blower hood which I could barely reach, and turn it back and forth to distribute the straw in the storage area below which was called the straw-mow. Dust and wheat chaff floated in circling fashion to the top of the barn so that I could barely see the rafters. My only breathing protection was a damp handkerchief over my mouth and nose which dried out quickly. With sweat dripping, it was dirty and tiring. I truly hated this filthy job and resented that that I was required to do something so difficult.

This day Mom, Grandma and Peggy prepared a large cooked meal. Two or three chickens were roasted in the summer kitchen. Mashed potatoes, green beans, creamed corn, squash and sliced tomatoes adorned the table. We fed the farmers who brought the threshing equipment and the neighbors who came to help out. Appetites were hearty.

Peaches were another major crop. The harvest of early fruit began in June and later varieties lasted until the end of September. Our orchard had about 500 trees of at least ten varieties. Getting a good crop of peaches required a fair amount of care beginning with a major pruning in March, spraying for insects and fungus four times beginning in late winter with the last one in September. No one enjoyed thinning the peaches because the peach fuzz was scratchy and got down your neck under your shirt. Clusters of fruit were so thick that we had to make a choice of which ones to leave on the tree. We did the chore when the peach was about the size of a marble, and often removing two and leaving only one on the twig to mature.

Even though the peaches were still fuzzy, picking ripe peaches was more fun, probably because an occasional peach snack made the work more appealing. The peach increased in size to a large degree during the last few days on the tree, so it was a close call on how long to let them ripen. If they got too large and soft, they spoiled quickly and sold for a lower retail value.

Mom took many truck loads of only peaches to the nearby grocery stores. Her sales ability was impressive and she always returned with an empty truck. By this time, Dad had another load picked for sale. Peaches were also quite popular on the peddle route as not many local farmers raised them.

FRUIT CELLAR

WHEN I WAS YOUNG THE FRUIT CELLAR, AS IT WAS called, was very intriguing. Since the steps were steep and rickety, us kids did not go down them until we were bigger. Why we called it the fruit cellar, I will never know. It was the storage area of many good foods—not just the fruit we kept there like cherries, peaches, plums, apples and raspberries.

Mom went down into the cellar and she always returned with lots of jars filled with an intriguing variety of foods in her arms. My mouth watered to see what she had chosen for supper. It seemed like the supply was endless, and I marveled at the many choices. This small room was separate from the main basement, and it did not have a door connecting them. It may have been an addition to the house as the original masonry bearing wall separated the two areas.

The only entrance to the fruit cellar was through a double door on the back porch floor. The doors going down were really not that obvious as they were painted gray, a good match with the rest of the floor. One had to take hold at the porch edge and lift up carefully. The steps were steep, and I sometimes gazed down into the dimly lit space.

When I was older, I was sent there often for food. I was surprised at how cool the room was, and I found it stayed pretty much the same temperature all year around. A single bulb in the ceiling with a string hanging from the socket provided the necessary light.

The compact room was only about fifteen by twenty feet, but it seemed much larger. On the right wall were shelves three feet deep running along the entire length for canned goods. The space was organized with separate sections for the many varieties of foods. It was quite colorful and looked like a beautiful picture. By the start of winter, the storage space was completely filled, and when spring and early summer arrived, only the empty shelves were seen.

In the far left corner, hooks in the floor joists above provided space for hams and bacons. At any given time, there may be as many as three or four bacon and ham sides hanging there. The ceiling was fairly low, so it was easy to reach out and touch the meat. We did not do the actual butchering, a nearby neighbor did it as a side business, but it was meat of the hogs from our farm. From each pig, we got two bacons, two hams, the stomach and trays of pudding (jellied head and organ meat cooked). All of this plus a large amount of sausage made from a mixture of cooked meat stuffed into the cleanly washed intestines.

Mom always did the ham cure process, vigorously rubbing a mixture of brown sugar, salt, pepper and salt-peter (a powdered preservative) for many days until there was a protective coating surrounding the meat.

The pig stomach was always used fresh. Known as "Hog Maw," rural folks considered it to be a delicacy. We stuffed it with carrots and potatoes plus other available vegetables and then oven roasted it until the stomach lining turned golden brown. This occasional menu item was one of our very favorites.

Immediately at the bottom of the steps, sauerkraut filled a very large—perhaps forty-gallon—crock. Mom took the best part of a day to make this unique mixture of shredded cabbage, salt and a touch of vinegar. She packed it in tightly with juices covering it completely so no air could enter, a circular wood covering it with handle pressed down firmly on top. This method allowed it to keep all winter into the spring. Whenever it was on the menu, Mom scooped some out and heated it. Oh, how wonderful it tasted on top of mashed potatoes with pork chops as the main entree.

A fifty-gallon lard can filled with animal fat sat next to the sauerkraut. This was our primary source of cooking oil, nearly everything fried used this lard. Large quantities disappeared every day as Mom used an ample amount for cooking. I can't think of a better tasting meal than crispy skin, chicken fried in deep lard, sweet potatoes also fried in lard and green beans cooked with ham.

A wooden cutting block about waist high sat next to the lard. On that old smooth-topped stump, we laid the large hams and bacons for slicing the needed amount for supper. A sharp knife rested on top of the block and came in handy and was used frequently.

A glance at the shelves straining with the canned harvest weight caused the realization that it was now the fall of the year and winter was not far away.

CATSUP MAKING

UPON THE ARRIVAL OF SEPTEMBER, THE WEATHER WAS beginning to change to fall and an excess of tomatoes remained in our large patch. Although we had been selling them all summer long, ours were the biggest and sweetest tasting on the market.

Looking at the remaining field of tomatoes, so many were still hanging on the vines that there was a red glow. The tomatoes were overripe, perfect for catsup making. Bill and I picked basketfuls and loaded them in the truck. Lots more remained and often the frost destroyed them before we could harvest any more. So we put the abundance to good use as quickly as possible.

Now was the time for Mom to make catsup for the winter ahead. The summer kitchen was waiting, the kettles ready and stove filled with kerosene oil for a long day of cooking. Soon, she began cooking on the old oil fire stove. Grandma Deimler was helping, busily removing the blanched tomato skins. A well worn wooden spoon stayed nearby for that necessary stirring, yet another task for Grandma.

The top shelf in the fruit cellar was still empty waiting for those bottles of catsup. The void caught one's eye as though the fruit cellar was a painting with an important part not yet completed. A good supply of other canned items filled the shelves below.

Mom, without recipe in hand, knew exactly how much of each ingredient gave the catsup its unique flavor. Mom cooked the tomatoes all day, simmering throughout the afternoon. She never timed them but knew when the catsup was the right thickness, ready to bottle.

Once the catsup was just right, it was left to cool down somewhat. Then, using a large dipper and a funnel, each bottle was filled carefully. Next came the capping process. Mom reserved this job for herself. She knew how much pressure to apply with the old bottle capper.

We had a large collection of bottles accumulated over many years, different shapes, sizes, wording and colors. While we never bought soft drinks, the assortment of bottles were from Coke, orange soda and root beer. I have no idea where these bottles came from. The top shelf of the fruit cellar was waiting for the almost-final addition.

The bottles with dual use in our family had already contained the summer's homemade root beer. Now they moved on to their next job as the containers for autumn catsup making. The long rows of bottles lined up on the shelves in the fruit cellar were a magical sight and certainly looked like they were home for the winter.

Once completed, the catsup cooled over night. The next day, we moved them to their spot in the fruit cellar where they awaited their trip to the Deimler kitchen table.

If I had to guess, at least one hundred and fifty bottles of catsup lined up on that reserved spot. At mealtime around the table, a familiar phrase sounded: "Pass the catsup, please." Sometimes we used a full bottle at one given meal.

The catsup making has continued in the Deimler family. Two daughters-in-law find making catsup to be pleasurable especially because of the special taste it brings to the meal.

Rita makes it for resale at the local farmer's market labeled with Mom's youthful photograph. Dian learned the recipe first hand from Mom, and cooks several batches of it each summer.

TURKEYS AND THE HOLIDAYS

Turkeys were our biggest cash crops. We raised about twelve hundred of them each year on the farm. A hatchery in Zanesville, Ohio sent the baby chicks in April. They were shipped in cardboard boxes with small holes on the top to allow the entry of fresh air. We knew they would be delivered by the mailman, so we watched each day with excitement as we awaited their arrival.

Prior to their coming, there was a flurry of activity to prepare the pens. We scrubbed them clean so the living conditions were as sanitary as possible. Turkeys were susceptible to diseases and cleanliness was very important. Then the "brooder stoves" were set into place and newspaper spread out on the floor with litter underneath. The papers were taken up daily and new ones put in place. Eventually the newspapers were no longer used and the older chicks were on the clean litter, a natural product we called "stays dry." Little feed trays and water dishes were filled and placed strategically. Turkeys were difficult to train to eat and drink, so it was critical that they could find the source quickly. We placed bright colored marbles in the dishes so that the baby turkeys would be attracted and pick at them. When doing so, they would get a taste of food or water and thus learn to take nourishment.

Mom took great care of the fragile birds so most baby turkeys lived through those first few days. Storms were of great concern as loud cracks of thunder sent the chicks scurrying to a corner of the room, piling one atop the other, sometimes so deep the bottom chicks were suffocated or crushed to death.

One evening about midnight, when were all asleep, there was a severe thunderstorm. Loud sounds were heard as the bolts of lightning gave a glow to the sky. We were all awakened suddenly and realized the eminent danger of our turkey flock. Now very much afraid, the young chicks were already piling in the corners as we raced through the rain to the turkey houses. I helped pull them loose and attempted to get them moving so that new breaths of life would take place. Luckily our quick action saved most of them. As the storm subsided, and now soaking wet from the torrential downpour, I returned to the farmhouse, hung up my clothes to dry and with visions of a job well done, soon fell back to sleep.

When the planes from the nearby Middletown Olmstead Air Force Base went into a thunderous dive creating a loud noise, it also caused a turkey pile up. Again we ran to the rescue!

Chickens carried the "black head" disease, so great care was needed so as not to transfer the disease as we went from the chicken to the turkey pen. Boots and shoes had to cleaned and disinfectant applied. One year the turkeys caught sinusitis. We had to catch every one so Mom could put a large penicillin capsule down the throat of each bird.

Uncle Paul Bashore had just begun a construction business following World War II and Dad employed him to build a new and modern turkey pen. When completed, it sat six feet above the ground with enough space to drive the tractor and manure spreader underneath, enabling us to load and haul droppings. The turkeys would be mostly on wire with half-inch openings with a hard surface floor where roosts were located in the back of the pens. This building was designed to house the entire flock. A ramp-way allowed entry to the building and a platform for walking continued along the front side where large trough-like containers were filled with grain and mash as well as trays of water.

The arrival of Thanksgiving, Christmas and to some extent New Years Day meant the farm was busier than ever. An advertisement announcing "dressed turkeys" for sale was placed in the Middletown Press and the Journal. Our party line phone rang frequently as the orders came in. Grandma Deimler wrote the name and desired weight in a black hard-cover notebook. From there, little white tags with strings carried the customer's name and actual weight for later delivery.

As teenagers, my brother Bill and I usually caught the live turkeys and killed them for cleaning. We placed the customer tags in our shirt pocket. As I looked over the flock sizing each carefully, I caught one that looked close to what the customer had in mind and then tagged it by attaching it to the bird's leg. The primary slaughtering area consisted of two poles with a metal rod between them. Hanging from the rod at three locations was a short chain with a swivel and snap on each. I bound my turkey by the feet with a loop rope and attached at least two to each snap. In this manner, up to as many as six turkeys could be killed at the same time. Holding the turkey's head and stretching it forward slightly, I applied the blade of our sharp knife quickly so as to make the inevitable as painless as possible.

An assembly line of tables and wash basins was set up in the garage. The various stations were staffed by ladies who lived nearby. Here they sat to work cleaning and preparing the birds for roasting. There was a small stove in the corner upon which sat a large old tub filled with water. It was kept at a ready-to-boil temperature. As I helped lift it from the stove, I was intrigued by the this old container made of copper that in some ways looked out of place in the turkey cleaning area and today would be considered a real antique. I never saw Mom use a thermometer, she knew exactly when the water was hot enough for dipping the turkeys. Each turkey was dipped in the hot water separately for a few minutes until the feathers pulled out easily. Care was given so as not to tear the skin.

The washing and gutting was almost like surgery. Much pride was evident as they were cleaned carefully. After the turkeys were prepared, they were placed in large tubs awaiting delivery. Normally, the Pennsylvania November and December weather was cold enough so that it was not necessary to add ice to the tub. On rare occasions when the weather was warmer than usual, icing the birds ensured their preservation.

The day before each Holiday, the turkeys were loaded onto the pickup truck, and Mom delivered each one to the customer's front door. It was a personal service unheard of currently.

After Christmas, a few were sold for New Year's Day and any remaining turkeys were kept until the end of January and then sold to a wholesale poultry processor. We also kept a few extra turkeys for ourselves. From Thanksgiving through February, roasted turkey was on our menu numerous times.

FARM DOG

WE HAD TWO DOGS ON THE FARM. THEY WERE REAL farm dogs. They lived outside and ran free. They never had a fence or a dog house, nor did they get invited into the house. Mike, our German Shepherd, and Bubbles, our Beagle, slept on the back porch except for the coldest of winter nights when they found refuge in the barn.

Bubbles could smell out a rabbit and got to go hunting often. She was a typical beagle, loved each one of us equally and just liked to "hang out." She belonged to everyone!

Mike tagged along wherever we went. Mike was the true watchdog and sounded the alarm whenever a stranger set foot on our property. We all felt safer because of his vigilance. He was especially protective of Mom. I saw him step between her and a visitor on many occasions and give a ferocious growl if the stranger moved too close.

One evening, we accidentally locked Mike in the upper level of the barn. The wooden barn siding had vertical boards with a small space between. That next morning we noticed Mike's head in full view through a "window" that didn't previously exist in the barn. He had chewed a hole the size of his head between the boards.

No matter where I went on the farm, hikes in the woods or on our trap line, Mike was near. Often as we walked the land, he eased up to me and took my hand in his mouth.

Each and every morning when we stepped out of the kitchen door, Mike appeared out of nowhere. He followed us as we went about our morning chores. Mike was not allowed to be in the turkey or chicken pens and waited outside the door until our jobs were done. He followed us into the barn and stayed close when we milked the cow and fed the mules.

Rats were a menace. They chewed anything in their path, destroying bags of mash and grain in addition to carrying disease through their droppings. Dad paid Bill and I a nickel for each rat we killed. Mike was a big part of the hunt. Often after dark, when the rats came out of their holes, we sneaked into the feed storage area and surprised the rats. Mike usually was quick enough to catch one and shake it vigorously. Sometimes we saw a rat tail at the edge of the hole, grabbed it with our bare hands and flipped it to Mike who made the kill. Our rat hunting trip was successful and it was clearly another source of income for me.

When Bill plowed the field, Mike would trail after the tractor, back and forth in the furrows. Sometimes when he got very tired he found a shady spot to lay and waited for the tractor to make the next round. Then off he went down the field, staying close.

One hot day in July, we cut the wheat. The tall golden stems bent over with the weight of the ripe grain. The cutting was done with a wheat binder, now an antique piece of equipment. It had a cutter blade that moved horizontally just above the ground, cutting off the wheat at the lower stem. The wheat then fell into a canvas, went up a ramp on the machine and eventually landed on the other side in a shock tied with binder's twine. Several of us followed behind and began picking up the bundles and stood them together in a large shock for additional drying.

On this day, Dad rode the binder while Bill pulled it with the tractor. Mike was busy chasing field mice in the area just beyond the cutter blades. Then it happened, so quickly. Mike let out a yelp. Bleeding profusely, he had gotten too close to the blades which cut his legs and hind quarter before Bill could stop the engine. The wound was nasty and jagged.

Mom grabbed some cloth, ran to the field, and applied a tourniquet to stop the bleeding. Our veterinarian, who made house calls, was summoned to come quickly. After many stitches, Mike was carried into the main basement where it was cooler. It did not look good and we all thought Mike was a goner. Now it was our turn to take care of him. Mom was his primary nurse as she cared for him by changing his bandages and bringing him fresh water and food. Days went by, and we all continued to fear the worst. After about two weeks, Mike began to struggle in an effort to stand. With Mom's help, he made it to the backyard. We knew then that he was going to be all right.

My memories of Mike are vivid and will remain with me always. When Mike was about the age fourteen, while he was walking along route 441, the country road past our farm, he was hit by a neighbor's pickup truck. It was not the first time he was hit by an auto, but it was his last. My brother and I buried him wrapped in burlap in the upper corner of the backyard.

THE UNPREDICTABLE
NATURE OF FARMING

THERE IS NO GUARANTEE THAT ALL WILL GO WELL IN THE somewhat unpredictable growing process. There are many uncontrollable variables in farming that affect the final outcome. A worried look on the face of a farmer means a less than successful harvest, caused by a summer drought, a wind and hail thunderstorm, too much rain at harvest time, insects on the plants, a predator killing the chickens or rats in the feed bin.

Most farm owners were prepared for some losses each year, but many were not able to recover financially from these happenings. A few even went bankrupt, while many borrowed money. Some neighbors chose to help each through the bad times.

While we experienced our share of tough times, we usually found a solution. When the wheat sprouted on the shock because of too much rain, we still did the threshing and gleamed a part of it. When the newly cut hay met with rainy days and did not dry thoroughly, we used it for animal bedding. When the hail hit the peach crop, we salvaged the better fruit and sold it at a discount. Mom canned more and the relatives benefitted because we shared the bruised and damaged fruit.

Cash flow was a tremendous challenge since the year-round income was dependent on crops as they became ready for harvest and were sold. With the only winter cash income being from eggs, it was often insufficient to pay all the bills. In late winter, my parents struggled to balance the income with expenses.

Mom and Dad often borrowed short term money from neighbor and friend, Mabel Harbold, who was the daughter of the Coble dairy farmers. They had a large, several generation, profitable farm, with a herd of about 35 cows. Their land was more than one hundred acres. Mabel, her two brothers and sister had all stayed on the farm as adults so it was truly a family operation. She was most willing to help and always got paid back with interest. I also borrowed money from Mabel to purchase a new car.

We traded "hours in the field" with the Coble family. The two brothers each often worked four hours to bring hay into the barn. This meant that Dad had to work a full day at their farm to pay them back in hours worked. My bother Bill, Mabel's son Junie and the elder Coble (quite up in years) each counted as one half the amount of time worked and so sometimes Bill went to their farm. This process was stressful for Dad because the Cobles always sent the two brothers, Junie and sometimes their father came along. Their hours accumulated quickly, and the payback was a challenge. I was not considered old enough to figure into the swapping of hours agreement, so I felt a bit left out.

Loss of poultry through illness can affect the final results ending in a financial loss. The blackhead disease in both chickens and turkeys is a most dreaded happening. It is very contagious, and turkeys are more susceptible to the infection. The parasite lives in the soil and chickens can be carriers as well, so we needed to be very careful going from the chicken to the turkey house. We had a small container of disinfectant outside each chicken pen door which we stepped into upon entering and leaving. We treated the pens with disinfectant which helped to avoid cross contamination.

The young Leghorn chickens were put in a hayfield range during the summer, and then brought inside when they started to lay eggs in the fall. One year we found dead chickens every day with a mysterious blood mark on heir neck. Dad was certain it was a weasel doing the dirty work. I had a regular assignments watching, with rifle in hand, from the nearby hill. Sure enough the weasel attacked at the same time in early morning and evening. The chicken was bitten and the blood sucked out quickly by the weasel. I took many a shot with my .22 caliber rife but they were just too fast. Finally, shooting with an accurate aim, the weasel was bagged. Traps were also set in the pathway under the fence which proved effective. A fox was caught by Bill with a special bait trap that truly put an end to the chicken deaths. The chickens were completely safe again. Our neighbor, who had offered a five dollar reward, happily paid us for our handiwork.

It seemed like we never caught up with all the work to be done. We welcomed help from two of Mom's siblings, her sister Lill and brother Chill. Lill came often and was a cheerful and capable helper in the house. After World War II, Aunt Lill and her husband Paul Bashore both came to work on the farm. Uncle Paul was paid to do a variety of carpentry jobs and built the modern turkey pen.

Uncle Chill worked in the fields harvesting the crops. I know that he was there pulling red beets the day I was born. He was often called to work when there was extra help needed, especially when we kids were too young to be of much assistance in the field. During the war, when Uncle Chill was a gunner on the USS Borie, he was wounded seriously in an attack by Japanese kamikaze planes just two days before the war ended. He spent many months in the hospital and for a period of convalescence upon his return he, Aunt Dot and their son Larry lived with us.

Food of all varieties was scarce with many folks unable to afford sufficient amounts. Mom and Dad cared deeply about the family by offering them a part time income as funds permitted, extra food when we had more than enough, gasoline when it was rationed in the nineteen forties and an extra chair around the table was always available. Neighbors who were sick or had a death often needed a helping hand with routine tasks. I remember times when Mom milked cows and Dad pitched hay for them.

Rural folks pitched in and gladly gave of themselves. They did it not because they were paid, not for swap hours, and not for praise. They did it because it needed to be done.

SKUNK HUNTING AND
TRAPPING WITH BILL

It was a bitter January winter in central Pennsylvania. Much snow covered the cold, cold ground. But, at last came a day of slight warming, just enough to feel the difference. The wind was not quite as chilling. A light fog caused by the more temperate air and the frozen earth gave a scary feeling to our nearly full moonlit farm land.

Bill looked at me and said, "Hey Tom, let's go skunk hunting!" It didn't take much to convince me and what a great way to get out and do something FUN! So we grabbed our .22 rifles, readied our carbide miner's lamps, called for Mike our ever present dog and off we went. Skunks usually came out on this kind of warmer night, and we knew it would be a productive evening.

Hunting and trapping of all types was very popular with farm boys. It was a good way to add income to our savings account, too. Bill and I always trapped for skunks, opossum and muskrats during the winter. At night, hunting skunks and opossums was another way to add furs to our catch. We trudged through the fields and woods on many a several-hour excursion trying to surprise and bag our prey.

The trap line was a lot more work which required strenuous hiking through the wooded areas and along the various nearby streams. The traps alone were quite heavy, plus the bait, hammer and stakes. When we found a well-worn animal trail, we'd set a bait trap just at the edge. The entrails from Friday chicken cleaning made an enticing snack for our quarry. An old vegetable crate turned upside down, with a hole in the end and the bait at the opposite closed end became an effective setting for a catch. Skunks and opossums were fairly easy to fool, so we were quite successful in our limited business venture. Muskrats were much more difficult to catch. They had the ability to side-step the trap spring. Along the bank of the stream was a good place to look for trail slides and when we found one a trap was carefully placed in a slightly lower spot. Muskrats either twisted off their leg or chewed it off to escape the iron trap jaws, so you had to get up early to check the line. We were out on the move long before daybreak, and well ahead of the time that we had to begin barn work.

On that skunk hunting night and just over the hill, on the back field, we saw two skunks. Bill wasted no time in sighting his rifle and bang, it was a hit. I shot and hit the other one. Our faithful dog, Mike, sprang into action almost immediately and moved quickly to finish the kill. He grabbed and shook the skunks vigorously. With necks broken, there was no doubt they were dead.

Having two skunks in the bag, we walked briskly to other parts of the farm. A visit to our neighbors, Mr. and Mrs. Wesley Lauver's beehives, found another skunk tapping the hives for a treat of delicious honey bees. Here we had a third kill for our night's work.

The Lauver's were a unique addition to our farm neighborhood with an array of wonderful products to sell. They had about ten two-story beehives, chickens, quail, guineas and goats. Crops included broom corn and a host of vegetables. Our properties adjoined on the southeast corner of our farm. Bill and I often hiked over to visit when we had a brief break in our farm chores. It was interesting to watch Mr. Lauver making much-in-demand brooms from his own crop of broomcorn. We bought many of his brooms over the years. Mr. Lauver built the neatest stone spring house where very cold water bubbled from the ground. This is where he kept the goat's milk, butter and cheese refrigerated. How cool it was to step inside the spring house on a hot summer day. One of Dad's favorites to eat was Lauver's raw honey taken directly from the honey comb, wax included. A piece about 8 by 12" was cut, wrapped in wax paper and several layers of newspaper tied neatly with string. For a few pennies, this was an inexpensive treat enjoyed by all of us.

Many years later, long after I had left the farm, completed college and was married with several children, I learned from Mom that Mr. Lauver had passed. Mrs. Lauver was still living, and resided at a Mennonite home near where my family and I lived in Waynesboro, Pennsylvania. My wife Shirley, having heard many stories about my experiences on the farm, suggested we visit Mrs. Lauver. What a joyous moment it was as we recalled times gone by. Even though we lived two miles away from the Mennonite home where Mrs. Lauver resided, she often walked to our house on West Main Street for a drop-in visit. She always carried a basket on her arm, and inside were fresh baked goodies to share!

Returning to the farm house and barn, all of us quite worn out, Mike made a move to rid himself of the strong odor from the skunks. In the barnyard was a large watering trough. Even though it was cold enough to freeze the water, we broke the ice each day and filled it with fresh water for the animals. At this point, Mike's usual maneuver was to jump into the water trough and submerge himself and paddle vigorously. He would then jump out as if to say "enough of that" and shake himself to shed the cold water and hopefully the odor as well.

Our catch was hung in the rafters of our wood shed where they promptly froze in the cold temperatures, preserving them until the end of the week. The Farmers Market was held on Friday evenings, when all the farm folks came to browse, and all day on Saturday. The market was a special outing for the youngsters. Friday evening we found the fur buyer there and ready to make purchases. Very little price discussion transpired, selling the furs between $1 to $2 each depending on how little white was visible. All black furs brought the highest amount of money.

Mike's bath in the barnyard was not something we could do. Once back to the house, Bill and I hung our blue bib-jeans in the back stairway and showered in the new bathroom upstairs, but the smell lingered. I guess our parents felt there were more important things to complain about than the pungent odors of the skunk hunt, though!

PIG MONEY

Dad was always very happy when it was time to go buy baby piglets. We knew it because he whistled the entire way there and back. Off we would go in the pickup truck to a nearby farm.

The buying of piglets was exciting for my brother, sister and me. For weeks, Dad would watch the Friday edition of the *Middletown Press and Journal* to see if nearby farmers were advertising piglets for sale. Upon arrival at the seller's farm, the owner and Dad entered into a long haggle about what they were worth. If the asking price was $5 a pig, Dad would say, "It is not too much for you to ask, but it is a lot more than I can pay," and then offer $3 a piglet. Back and forth they would go until finally they would settle on $4 each.

Into the back of our pickup truck the piglets went and then the ride to the farm. Dad didn't whistle very often, but I did I love to hear him on pig buying trips!

There were six large pens which kept our total capacity to 24 pigs. One half of each pen was under roof and the other half exposed to the weather. We worked hard to get them ready including a fresh cleaning and spreading new straw. The little piglets squealed with delight as they were released to their new home.

The "mother pig" normally gave birth to a litter of about eight, sometimes as many as ten or twelve. The piglets were ready for fattening at six to eight weeks. Many farmers sold them to another farmer to grow them for butchering. We were in the business of buying baby pigs and then selling them to a butcher when they reached close to 200 pounds. They would sell for close to 20 to 25 cents per pound, meaning that the sale of 24 pigs represented a gross income of about $1000 to $1200.

My share for two pigs was close to $50 each, or a total of $100. Dad never subtracted the cost of purchasing the piglets or the cost of raising them so we were able to bank the total $100. When we were very young, Dad told Bill, Peggy and me that there were two pigs for each of us and when they were sold, the money would go into our savings account. Bill and I were to save for college and Peggy for establishing herself in her own home.

Knowing we'd be earning and saving money for our efforts on the farm made raising pigs a lot more palatable. Dad always fulfilled his promise and we all felt proud to watch our savings grow. In those days, folks kept track of their money in a little red savings account pass book. Ours was kept at the Middletown Citizens Bank and Trust Co. Taking the actual cash to the bank and placing it on the counter for the teller was a big day and in the process. We learned a lot about being thrifty!

Like all aspects of farming, raising pigs was a rigorous daily task. The early morning barn-work included preparing a breakfast composed of wet-mash for the pigs. "Mash" consisted of ground wheat, corn and oat grains mixed with water. This was poured into the trough for the pigs to eat. After they ate, we filled their trough with water. In the evening, we fed the pigs their supper. Added to the same mash, were buckets of skim milk hauled in wooden barrels from the nearby dairy. Several ears of corn on the cob was given to the pigs and was considered a real treat by the pig family. Feeding the pigs was called "slopping the pigs."

The pigs grew rapidly, reaching close to fifty pounds by the age of twelve weeks. Now it was time for a job I did not like at all. Castration was necessary to develop the best quality meat in males. My job was to help catch the pigs for the veterinarian. Just picture chasing a pig that does not want to be caught, and you will have some idea of the difficulty of doing so. Once we had them, we held them by their rear legs with belly side towards the vet. With a quick cut, the veterinarian removed the testicles, applied sulfa powder and a covering of tar. The vet's sense of humor was to make a dinner menu suggestion followed by a hearty laugh. We did not think his joke was very funny.

Cleaning the pig pens was also a distasteful job. The strong odor of pig manure was so strong, it burned our nostrils. The pens were kept clean with the dirt shoveled out every week. Clean straw was put on the floor inside, and the open, outside area left bare. Grandma asked us to remove our clothing and bathe immediately upon completion of this chore.

One particular summer, Dad decided to expand the pig business. The concept was to pasture them in the late spring about the time school was out for the summer and fatten them by year end. A spot near our property corner and next to the woods was selected. Fencing was carefully installed by Dad and his cousin Wilmer, who periodically worked on our farm. It was important to get the fence bottom touching the ground so the pigs could not escape. Twenty five additional piglets were bought, doubling our herd. The project quickly soured with the little pigs using their small nose to edge their way under the fence. It wasn't long before a hole appeared large enough to provide them the opportunity to run free. The next few weeks our phone rang constantly with neighbors calling to alert us to where we could find the escaped pigs. I believe those pigs visited just about every neighboring farm, and herding them home was mostly a chase!

Raising pigs became more fun when it became a part of our 4-H club activity. One morning, our one-room school was filled with excitement as Miss Demey announced that the Dauphin County Agriculture Agent would be holding a 4-H organizational meeting later that week, right here in our own school. Parents were invited and we were thrilled to see both Mom and Dad attend the meeting, a rare occasion.

Bill, Peggy, and I joined and became active in 4-H. Of course, my first project was pig raising, with chickens and gardening to follow later. We were given 4 by 6" notebooks where precise entries were kept on the business of raising pigs. Costs, quantities of food, weights and care were recorded meticulously. With the help of the thoroughly outlined booklet, guidance of the county agent and Dad's help, our 4-H venture was a success. For the next five years, my 4-H experience continued by helping me to learn how to plan, budget and organize a project. Monthly meetings were held at the school house, each one beginning with this pledge:

> I pledge my HEAD to clearer thinking,
> my HEART to greater loyalty,
> my HANDS to larger service,
> and my HEALTH to better living,
> for my club, my community, my country and my world.

Our Motto: To make the best BETTER.

In six to seven months, in spite of the hard work of raising pigs, they reached the weight of 200 pounds and were ready for slaughter. This also meant I was able to add to my savings account. With the additional money I earned from fur trapping, killing farm rats and hiring out to neighboring farms I had a total savings of close to $1600 by the time I graduated from high school. This was enough to pay for my first two year's tuition and first year of board at Penn State.

I never thought that much about the pig money until many years later. There must have been times when Mom and Dad were short of cash and really could not afford to make good on their promise. But, we always got our share of the money when the pigs were slaughtered.

Chicken coops

Disc to toil soil; Horse-drawn cultivator; John Deere Crawler

Opposite, Top: Farmall A Tractor; Middle: Hay bailer;
Bottom left: Hay wagon; Bottom right: Hay dump rake.

Above: Plowing the field; Threshing machine for wheat

Above: Wheat and grain seed drill; Wheat combine.

Free-range for chickens and coop

Turkeys in raised pens

A HOUSE CALL

UNHEARD OF IN TODAY'S WORLD, A DOCTOR OFTEN MADE a house call in the 1930's and 40's. Mom and Dad never went to a doctor's office for just a check up and such a trip was extremely rare for my siblings and me. One had to be really sick to be seen by a physician simply because there was just no money to pay the bill. Health insurance did not exist in those times.

There were a few occasions when the doctor made a call to the farm to examine Bill, Peggy or me and at least one time or two for Mom or Dad. The era of antibiotics was years ahead, so when you got an upset stomach or a chest cold, it was a tough time until you were well again.

One January, I began with just a head and chest cold that got worse as the days moved along. The usual cough treatment was a half of lemon on which you sprinkled some salt and licked the juice. This often slowed down the coughing but certainly was not a cure for the cold itself. The Vicks jar was the source of medication for unclogging the breathing, but never lasted long into the night. Having a cold in the depth of winter was about as miserable a feeling as one could have.

I was ten years old, and sleeping in the bedroom above the kitchen. The good news was that the heat from the kitchen stove rose up through the open grating in the floor and the warmth helped keep me comfortable. Lying in bed, in the quiet, I remember the soft pattering of snow and sleet hitting the tin roof above.

I was sick and my cough was a deep croup. Mom had that serious look on her face, one of concern for her little boy. I could hear the muffled conversations in the kitchen below. It was certain the discussion was about whether the doctor should be called. A house call was always a last resort, even though the cost could be only two or three dollars. Sufficient funds were scarce enough to cause much discussion.

Therefore, next came the muster plaster treatment, a last trial to knock out a bad chest cold. The kitchen cabinet was filled with cotton cloths made from the bags in which wheat flour or animal feed was purchased. In the medicine chest was a tin container of dry mustard powder. The mustard plaster ingredients were a mixture of water, mustard and flour. A paste was made and spread thickly on the cotton cloth, then covered with a clean cloth. Lots of heat was generated by this combination, but Mom always warmed it just a bit more in the wood stove oven.

The mustard plaster was placed on the chest with lots of blankets on top. I could feel the heat penetrating my body and the perspiration began. There was some danger of serious skin burns so the application had to be checked periodically to make certain there were no blisters. After twenty minutes or so, the plaster was removed. Sometimes Mom applied Vicks or lard to the chest and then you turned over for a treatment to the back.

Many folks claimed this to be the ultimate cure for a bad chest cold and it often was effective. However, this was one of those times it did not help. With the fear of pneumonia in mind, Mom and Dad had another talk and the doctor was phoned.

He was a big man, Dr. Rife Gingrich, MD, towering at least six feet and two inches, weighing close to two hundred pounds. He was obviously in excellent physical condition as he bounded up the back stairway not even breathing hard.

Both his size coupled with his pleasant demeanor caused me to feel at ease immediately.

Dr. Gingrich had a large group of patients in Middletown that included a general practice, surgery and delivery of babies, as well. He was a new physician for us as the doctor who delivered me had an over extended list of clients and found it difficult to come when the need was greatest.

With a smile and a "how you feeling young man," he immediately began to listen to my chest. However, my interest was not his large hands or his stethoscope, it was the beautiful big black medicine bag he had placed on the nearby chair. There is no other way to describe it than beautiful, as it seemed to be the shiniest leather, as black and smooth as I had ever seen. The bag was wide at the bottom and tapered smaller near the top. The handles were protruding and appeared to be too large and out of proportion with the overall size.

By now, he was talking to Mom, as Dad had remained in the kitchen below. "His chest sounds pretty bad," he said to her, "and it could perhaps be pneumonia. I will give you some cough syrup to break it loose and some medicine that will help."

He opened the big black bag with a quick jerk. As he pulled each handle so as to spread the top apart, trays of medicine appeared. They popped up as if to jump out of the bag. There were long thin glass tubes each filled with pills of a variety of colors.

Reaching into one corner he pulled out a small paper envelope and poured in a generous amount until the envelope was bulging. In the bottom of the bag he secured a medium sized bottle of cough syrup. Writing my name and instructions on a glue backed label, he licked it, and applied it to the bottle.

Parting with a word of *get well*, he left as quickly as he entered. Dad, with an anxious look, was relieved to learn that one dollar this time was all that was charged. It would have normally been more, but the good doctor was also alert to the economy of the times and charged just enough to cover the cost of the medicine and gas to make the trip.

The instructions for me were lots of bed rest, drink ample fluids, cough syrup and—to my chagrin—continue the mustard plasters.

HERSHEY HIGH SCHOOL

IT WAS AN INTIMIDATING DAY FOR A COUNTRY KID AS I walked across the parking lot to enter Hershey High School. The ten miles from home was the furthest distance from the farm that I had traveled before. I was certain that everyone had their eyes fixed on me as I approached the front door. The building was gigantic. A steady flow of students arriving from the nearby rural area were in the same situation I was in, and probably experiencing similar emotions.

My education in the one room school had ended at the close of eighth grade. We were required to take a county test to transition to high school, ninth grade. Having ranked second in Dauphin County scoring, I received lots of congratulations.

We said "so long" to our country friends, some of whom we never saw again. Harry Shope followed in the steps of his brothers who now had their own farms, and after eighth grade he went on to work with his dad, eventually assuming responsibility for the original farm. Other neighbors stayed in touch, while some rode with my brother and me to school in the 1948 Pontiac that Dad bought when Bill first went to high school.

My jitters passed eventually, as I quickly found I was well prepared for high school. I made new friends easily. As the results of tests given to ninth grade students, I was moved from academic into the college preparatory section. This decision was preceded by a parent and student conference with the school dean, and both of my parents attended. In Dad's mind, I was well on my way to college even though only a high school freshman.

In physical education class, having learned to swing a bat earlier, I enjoyed the softball games we often played. In the winter, we had swimming class, a new experience for me. Because of the fear of Polio, most kids had never been in a public pool and had very little skill as a swimmer. I became unafraid of water and took a great deal of pleasure learning how to stay afloat and becoming proficient in the different swimming strokes.

Hall Patrol was the most prestigious club for guys in the school. The Hall Patrol got out of every class a few minutes early with each member being assigned a strategic hall position. We were very much in control of student flow throughout the building which played an important role in safety. Membership was nominated and voted upon within the club. It was a happy day when I learned in the beginning of my sophomore year I had become a member. My transition to High School was now complete.

Another club I joined that year was Hi-Y for boys. It included guys who were interested in service to the school. The program was sponsored by the YMCA, and had an emphasis in Christian living, good character and responsibility. I was later elected to the leadership position of Secretary of the twenty-five member group. Our slogan was "live pure, speak true, right wrong."

My social experience began when the girl's booster club held it's winter dance during my junior year. It was a Sadie Hawkins Dance, and I was in a state of shock when a cute young lady invited me to be her date. In a nervous response, I said, "But I do not know how to dance." "I'll teach you," she said, and after only one day of reflection, I agreed. The plan was for me to go to her home after dinner for several nights of lessons. It was obvious she had a crush on me and that gave me even more apprehension. It did turn out to be a fun time and after about three lessons, I was declared ready to be her dancing partner. A new door opened in my life.

Also, in my junior year, I was asked to become the school newspaper's Sports editor which, after discussions at home, I accepted. It was determined that before going to the games, I would come home after school and take care of my chicken and animal responsibilities. Sports editor was a major job, and I was expected to cover all sports activities both home and away.

Some of the students helped in covering games, but I attended most events and especially every football and basketball game during my senior year. Harry traveled with me. Dad supported this commitment with the generous use of his car, providing gasoline from the farm gas supply. I also reported for the *Harrisburg Patriot News* by calling in the results from the nearest phone booth. At the end of the season, I was paid one dollar per game for my services.

As a senior, my responsibilities expanded to also become sports editor for the yearbook, *Chocolatier 1952*. This was a very enjoyable experience as it was not only fun, but the staff was made up of the true "in crowd." I was good friends with the editor and all who worked on the yearbook.

Each year the students had a day to hold the various school positions, including the principal and teachers. Both my junior and senior year I applied for and received the opportunity to be the algebra teacher. It was invigorating and fun to serve in this role. A desire to teach has remained with me.

In early June 1952, as graduation approached, I realized my life was about to change drastically. I had just applied to enter Penn State University's School of Forestry, and had been accepted. The farm was sold that spring and we moved to our new home about six weeks earlier.

SUMMER LOGGING

THE SUMMER OF 1953 WAS A UNIQUE AND FORMATIVE experience for me. It was a part of my transition from the rigors of farming.

During my freshman year in college, forestry students were given the opportunity to accept summer employment at various locations mostly in the western United States. Some went with the US Forest Service and others with private companies. I noticed on the campus bulletin board an announcement for Weyerhaeuser Timber Company. They wanted "choker-setters." "Must be in good physical condition," said the ad. But what caught my eye was the pay, at $2.12 per hour with room and board included. That was far better than employment with the US Forest Service and I needed college money. So I applied and was accepted.

My employment letter confirmed the details and specified a June date to report in Longview, Washington. This correspondence required me to have a pair of corked boots, leather gloves, work clothes and suspenders (belts not allowed). I had no idea of the job description of a choker setter, and only found out later how extremely dangerous it was.

My best friend George and I rode together with his parents to Chicago, home of his grandparents. From there he took a bus to northern Montana for a Forest Service job and I took my first ever airplane trip from Chicago to Portland, Oregon. Longview is located close to Portland just across the Columbia River in south western Washington.

On Sunday evening I arrived at the specified local train station where I soon found that other choker setters and loggers met each week. We all boarded a train, and with no information on where we were going, the train ambled deep into the dense hemlock and pine forests of that area. It seemed like a long trip as it wound along a sparkling, rapidly moving mountain stream and must have been at least fifteen to twenty miles from town. The train was the only way to reach the logging site which turned out to be a sprawling camp located in a valley area, with that same beautiful stream running through it.

Little two-person cabins dotted the landscape. They were about twelve by twenty feet in size with a small single bedroom on each end and a middle section with a wood heating stove and two chairs. Outside showers and primitive toilet facilities reminded me of the farm.

In the middle of the camp was a large dining hall with rectangular tables and benches. A huge kitchen adjoined. Extra tables lined the one wall along the window where, I later learned, you picked up your lunch in the morning. "Flunkies," as they were called, cooked and waited on tables. They also took care of other such domestic services as laundry and cleaning. The meals were served home style with a never ending flow of a large assortment of foods. Loggers were non-communicative and meal conversation was limited to passing the food and talk about the weather or work.

My roommate was old, salty and extremely quiet. I heard very little from him, except I was awakened in the early morning by his deep cough followed by a rather annoying spitting into a cup while sitting on the edge of his bed. Luckily, I met Richard, a young forestry engineer graduate of the University of Washington who came from Seattle. He traveled to the logging camp from home each week and returned on the weekend to his wife and small daughter. His job was to survey and map the areas to be logged. He helped to work out a switch in cottage assignments and the two of us were roommates the rest of the summer.

In the morning, we arose early with breakfast promptly at 6 a.m.—another thing to which I was accustomed. It was a typical hearty meal. I noted a large pile of sandwiches and a variety of fresh fruit and cake on the extra tables by the window.

Loggers were lined up filling their lunch buckets or paper bag. Large tanks with a spigot on the bottom contained milk and were used to fill an assortment of brown whiskey bottles. I did not have one, but a kind, bearded logger offered to bring one for me the next morning. The brown bottle, he said, would keep the milk from spoiling and I should find a cool shaded spot or stream to put it in when we arrived at our work location. Having drank raw milk on our farm, this was my first taste of pasteurized milk. I used that same brown bottle all summer and left it there when I departed.

Immediately after breakfast, we boarded a large truck with benches on the back, again not a new experience for me. From the camp, we rode into the deep woods where the cutters had already felled hemlock, spruce and pine trees that were two feet or more in diameter. Western forests are mostly on steep terrain, and this area was quite hilly with ravines filled with beautiful streams and sizable timber.

Logs cut into twenty foot lengths lay crisscrossed along the hillside. At the top was a steam engine anchored securely. An attachment of about four 2" steel cables hung from a main line that extended to the bottom of the hill where a pulley was attached to a tree stump. Our crew had four choker setters including the foreman who also set a choker each time.

The choker drop-lines dangled from the main cable and the engine operator slacked the line, lowering the shorter drop lines so each setter could grab hold of one. On the very end of the cable was a knob which fit into a slip-slide piece. My job, and each of the others, was to select the closest log, throw the cable around it and insert the knob into the slip piece which choked up tightly against the log. A large horn sounded from the steam engine at the top of the hill and the logs came out with frightening force. When the signal to pull the logs was given, the foreman watched carefully while we all jumped or ran on adjacent logs to be in safe territory. At the top, the logs were lifted by crane onto trucks and hauled to be loaded unto the train.

Safety was very important to Weyerhaeuser Timber Company. Choker setting is termed as one of the most dangerous jobs there is, anywhere. Men can be crushed between logs, bones broken and sometimes they lose their lives in this formidable occupation. I believe my days in the farm fields, often equally dangerous, prepared me for this particular time in my life. The true danger of choker setting never really worried me, and happily our crew had a positive safety record that summer.

My friend Richard and I developed a close relationship. His career was much like what I pictured myself doing. We had some long talks about future possibilities. The camp remained open on weekends for those who had no other home and so by choice I spent my open time in camp hiking and fishing. On one particular Friday, I traveled with him to Seattle and spent a wonderful time with him and his family.

I had learned to trout fish while a freshman at college and it was becoming a favorite pastime. The streams near the camp, I happily learned, were filled with trout. Mom mailed my fly rod to me about the second week after I arrived. Many evenings and weekend side trips into the woods found me with rod in hand landing a beautiful mountain trout.

The logging operation closed two weeks in July for vacation. During that period, I accepted a job to be on fire watch in a nearby camp. They gave me a supply of food and I spent two wonderful weeks keeping an eye on the property. My spare time was spent with my fly rod, fishing and hiking nearby. I was alone during that time but was not aware of any dangers.

The summer went by quickly. Pay checks were mailed home un-cashed and Mom deposited them in the bank for my college savings. My food and shelter were provided for, and the small amount of money I brought along was sufficient for any personal needs.

Mom and Dad had never seen the western part of the country. At my suggestion, they decided to take an extended vacation, leaving the Sunoco station in the good hands of Dad's assistant. They traveled westward, taking in the sights for the first time. My sister Peggy traveled with them.

They picked me up in Longview in late August. We traveled from there going east along the Columbia River that runs between Oregon and Washington. The valley and river views were spectacular.

I had arranged to pick up George on the return trip. We side-tracked into upper Montana to meet him. Happily, we found him having had a great summer job with the US Forest Service.

RELIGION IN OUR FAMILY

FARMING CERTAINLY GIVES ONE AN OPPORTUNITY TO WITness the cycle of life up close. Many crops, fruit trees and berries appear to be lifeless in the winter, yet return to new being in the spring. Seeds sprout when placed in fertile soil and young leaves appear on hardened twigs, all signs that there is a sequence of death and new life that many folks feel will happen even though we do not understand the process completely.

One who toils the earth and sees this evolution first hand must certainly believe there is a higher power. A farmer whose very existence depends on springtime needs no greater evidence in order to feel secure as one who believes in God.

Religion in the Deimler farm family is somewhat convoluted. Defining our belief follows a complex trail. Dad and Mom certainly believed in God, but there was not a strong evidence of their religious foundation as a part of our upbringing. Both Dad and Mom's parents prayed, looked to a higher power for strength and reflected strong faith through their words and actions. My parents displayed much the same example.

Yet in my early years, we did not worship nor attend church as a family. Grandmother Deimler was an active church person and her daughter, who lived nearby, would come by regularly and take her to The Church of God in Middletown.

Although she did not wear a bonnet, she pulled her hair back much like the background of her own parents. Somewhere along the way, our Mennonite neighbors invited the three of us kids to attend Sunday School and Church with them. Nearly every Sunday they picked us up in their all-black automobile and we worshipped at their church with their family. Here women sat on one side in the church while the men sat in a separate area across the aisle.

When I was about 12 years old, there was a religious revival held in Harrisburg. Our teacher invited those students interested in going to attend with her. She drove us to a large auditorium where there must have been more than 1000 people in attendance. At the closing of the service, there was an "Altar Call" and both Bill and I went down to profess our life to Christ.

Miss Demey talked to Mom and Dad about that happening. This experience became the beginning of a new religious time for our family. Grandma asked her preacher at the Church of God to come visit us at the farm. Dad was a bit skeptical regarding his view of clergy and so was not fond of the idea. Shortly after the invitation to drop by, the Reverend made a call and soon warmed up to Dad. The bonding point in this new relationship began when the Pastor asked whether he could dig in the manure pile to find little red fishing worms. Dad immediately offered him a pitchfork and was amazed to see him roll up his sleeves and go to work digging and reaching into the pile to pick up the worms.

Before long, I learned that our entire family would be attending several confirmation meetings in preparation for baptism. On Easter of that year, all five of us were baptized by submersion in a large water tank in front of the altar. Three times we were each dipped and then pronounced saved through the blood of Jesus Christ.

While I enjoyed attending there, the formality of worship services was not something for which Dad liked, so in a few years he became less active and eventually stopped attending altogether. However, I never doubted Dad's faith. It was renewed for me many times as various harvests drew near. Severe thunderstorms were a menace for farm crops and I saw him stand by the kitchen window watching a wind-, rain- and hail-filled storm. Perhaps it was just before peach harvest and as he gazed out with his head bowed ever so slightly, I knew he was uttering a prayer to One more powerful than himself.

On Sundays at noon, Dad liked to listen to the religious services from the Mormon Tabernacle in Salt Lake City. We all enjoyed the beautiful music from the choir. The highpoint of the program was a segment, "The Spoken Word," by Richard Evans and at that moment, precisely 12:20 pm, we all knew to be still and quiet. The sermonette was short, about six minutes, but it was powerful and left a positive thought for the week ahead.

Mom stayed active in church for a longer time but also stopped attending at some point. She was the focus of what we all believed, and suggested prayer as a way to find hope. Mom always did the prayer at mealtime. The only phrases I still remember are, "Thank you Lord for every good and perfect gift," and "Feed our souls in the bread of life."

Meanwhile, Bill drove the three of us children to church with Grandma, and sometimes Mom. The Church of God played a key role in what I believe and it continues to guide me in many ways. I stayed active and participated with the Sunday evening youth fellowship throughout my high school years. The program groups were mostly religious discussions on a relevant topic. There was always plenty of conversation around the table followed by refreshments. College vacations found me returning there often.

The two religious holidays we celebrated were Easter and Christmas. At Easter we decorated eggs. We dipped them in solid colors and on occasion we had food color tubes and decorated them by hand. An Easter basket was special and sometimes contained a piece of chocolate in addition to jelly beans and the hard boiled eggs we had painted. We attended church at that time and were taught that the death and resurrection of Christ was the focal point of our Christian belief.

Christmas was a time of lots of fun and excitement that began after the last turkey was cleaned and delivered. We believed the birth of Jesus to be on December 25th and that message was an important focus. The Christmas tree came from our neighbor's farm and usually had crooked branches and uneven pruning. We spent many hours getting the old series wiring of the tree lights to work because if one went out, the entire string of lights went dark.

Gifts mostly comprised things we needed like shirts, jeans and socks. Our Christmas stocking was filled with hard candy, English walnuts and an orange. My biggest thrill was that Santa Claus was found asleep on our sofa several times. Many years later, I knew it was Dad who was there for us. Dad continued his Santa Claus role for years beyond and included the grandchildren and even neighbor kids after our children were older.

My activity in church continued beyond the farm, while in college. In the military I was active at the Chapel at Fort Knox, including teaching Sunday School. Beyond discharge from the military, I married my college sweetheart, Shirley Swisher and we continued our faith and belief which we shared with our children.

Though my religious background is varied and the influences were many, I formed a strong personal faith. As I reflect on my belief, I realize that for a long time I have been influenced by a feeling of the Spirit within. As a young person, it was clear in many situations on the farm. As I grew older, I felt there was an urging coming from inside myself that was giving guidance to my actions. My belief in many ways was molded by my deeply religious grandmother. Her teachings became very much a part of my early life.

Progressing through college and beyond, I continued to listen for that internal voice. Sometimes it was very strong and there was no doubt that I could hear the message. At other times, it was faint and I almost had to strain to get even the slightest idea of what I should be doing.

I know with all my heart that much of what I achieve in this world is because within me, the Spirit flowing from a Higher Power is causing me to stop, listen and then take action.

Free

The squirrel on high is oh so free,
Jumping on branches and peeking at me.
I often wondered how it would be,
If I were a squirrel looking at me.

What would I see, Oh what would I see,
A life of contentment, surely that's me.
Caring and serving in the grand scheme of things
Reaping rewards that happiness brings.

A faith and belief in One so Supreme
And a fifty year mate, how short it does seem.
With family now grown
Living full lives of their own.

If I were that squirrel, high on the run
Jumping on branches and having much fun,
I'd say with a smile while looking to see
That guy on the ground, he is free just like me.

by Thomas R. Deimler

EPILOGUE

My EARLY YEARS WERE QUITE DIFFERENT THAN THOSE of my adult life or those of my own children. Each span of time in one's life notches significant milestones reflecting that generation. For me, the hard-earned values I learned on the farm have become a way of life.

The transition to a new lifestyle after the farm years and high school graduation was relative easy. I turned eighteen years of age that summer. It was good to work for a neighbor in the fields. However, anticipation of entering the School of Forestry at Penn State was foremost in my mind.

It was everything I had imagined and even more. College was stimulating and exciting. I made some lifetime friends and one of them, George Weimer, married my sister Peggy. As a Dean's List student and a sophomore, I was invited to go into the Wood Utilization course, still in the forestry, but a major in wood products engineering.

My pig money savings was being put to good use, getting me off to a good start and no worries initially about tuition and board. During my second year, I began work as a waiter in the girl's dining room which earned a meal for me in return. Along with my summer work and part time employment with the university research department, I was able to meet all expenses, working my way through college.

My two close friends, George Weimer and Pete Davis, and I rented various rooms or an apartment, rooming together for most of the years at school. An old high school friend, Dave Bucher, joined with us for one semester. Dave and his girlfriend, Betty, set up a blind date for me, introducing me to, Shirley Swisher, who soon became my steady girlfriend. She provided a new dimension of excitement to my life that I had not experienced previously. Both she and Betty were studying at Polyclinic Hospital in Harrisburg to become registered nurses.

Graduation was in June 1956, the year I cast my presidential vote for Dwight Eisenhower. The speaker at commencement referred to the old cliché, "life is a destination," "but one cannot be like a ship afloat at sea with no compass or course. Set goals," he said and "sail towards your objectives."

I landed a super job with Duquesne Light Company in Pittsburg at an annual salary of $4800, the second highest in the graduating class. My job was related to their wood utility poles and involved research into various issues of inventory and replacement. The big city life was not what I wanted at this point in time though, so I was, in a way, happy to receive my military draft notice that November, 1956.

Army basic training was at Fort Benning, Georgia a somewhat barren track of southern sand. Upon completion, I was assigned to Fort Know, Kentucky in the artillery division. Only one person was sent to Korea since that war had wound down and the war in Vietnam had not yet begun. I felt fortunate not to have been sent to foreign soil and subsequent military action.

During my time at Fort Knox, I was invited to teach the Forestry merit badge to the local boy scouts. I found this to be very interesting and helping as a volunteer appealed to me. Here I met a full time scout professional who recommended that I consider a position with the Boy Scouts of America. My immediate plan upon completion of my military obligation was to get married and return to Penn State for graduate work, so working for the Boy Scouts did not seem like a viable option. However the thought of a Scouting career was planted in my mind.

On November 22, 1958, I married Shirley Ann Swisher of Elizabethtown, Pennsylvania. We honeymooned in the Pocono Mountains, returning to our homes for Thanksgiving. Next, it was on to Penn State to pursue a graduate education.

Shirley had her RN degree and became employed locally while I was registered in grad school beginning in February. In the meantime, I became involved with the boy scout troop at the Methodist Church in State College. A visit with the local district executive of the scouts and my interest in becoming a full time professional with the Boy Scouts of America became intense. There was a certain feeling that this is where my life was pointing and before long I was completing an application. The masters degree program at Penn State was put on hold.

My first assignment was in Waynesboro, Pennsylvania with the main office in Hagerstown. It was a challenging career and the demand upon our young married relationship was significant. We had a new baby in 1959, Tom Jr, and this made our family and work lifestyle even more difficult. Another son, Stephen, came a little over two years later, in 1961.

A move with the Scouts took us to Washington, DC and then to Baltimore where our third son, Michael, was born in 1964. My busy schedule was even more rigorous at this time and we worked hard to make both family and career succeed! My annual salary was limited at $6300 in 1965. We had to plan our budget well and make every penny count.

A significant series of promotions came during our time in Baltimore which continued through 1974, when I became the council Scout Executive (Executive Director) in Gastonia, North Carolina. Shirley had been employed part time with Baltimore County as a public health nurse. She continued her own career working as volunteer coordinator with Hospice in Gastonia. She also completed her education for a bachelor's degree through St. Joseph's College in Maine. By this time Tom and Steve were in college and Mike was finishing high school.

My career with Scouting was on a good track, and having served well as the Scout Executive for nearly five years, plus six years as area director in North Carolina, I received another opportunity. In 1986 I accepted the position of Council Executive in Tampa, Florida giving direction to the program to fifteen thousand youth and a two million dollar budget. Shirley again moved to a new challenge, that of Asthma and Allergy Director for Florida.

My last promotion with the Boy Scouts was in 1995 when I became National Director of the Relationships Division. In this role, I traveled throughout the country representing the scouting organization and it's aims and goals to the various chartering organizations.

At the first of 2000, retirement seemed the appropriate decision. Now my life would take on yet another perspective. My love of young people has prevailed. Since the beginning of my retirement, I have continued to serve as a substitute teacher and part time math teacher in several high schools. I find it invigorating and rewarding to work with the future leaders of our great country.

All three of our sons have wives and their own families. Tom, Jr had an earlier marriage to Sherry Jones with two children, Alex and Trey. Tom is now married to Joy Zambrano and living in California with two small children, Enrique and Cruz plus Joy's daughter, Arielle. Steve is married to Rita Stancavage, living on a small farm in Hurdle

Mills, North Carolina. Mike is married to Dian Sokolowski and they have a son, Jake, and a daughter, Jessie. They also have an adopted son, Jeff Connell. They own a small farm property near Atlanta.

After fifteen years, my retirement continues to be a joyous time for me. My passion for the earth prevails and there is always time for me to put my hands into the soil. I will forever find pleasure in looking for the sprouts of new seeds to peep through the ground.

Straight Rows farming has made a positive impact upon me permanently. The lessons of the land were learned well and guide me still.

ACKNOWLEDGMENTS

HEARTFELT THANKS TO MY DAUGHTER-IN-LAW, DIAN. With me every step of the way, she provided much encouragement, editorial expertise and overall guidance. This book would not be possible without the countless hours of support she gave so freely.

I wish to express my gratitude to the many folks who gave me a helping hand along the way to becoming an adult. All lived near our farm and include: The Coble family; Wesley Lauver and wife Flora; Harry Espenshade; Mildred Strayer and Squire; Henry Longnecker and parents; and Eli Shope.

Sincere thanks to my constant companions, Harry Shope and Junie Harold for many hours of fun and enduring friendship.

Thanks to Jeff Connell for his tireless reading and editing of the draft copy.

A word of appreciation to my wife of 56 years, Shirley. Her support during the many hours I worked on this book as well as her inspiration throughout were very helpful. Thank you, my partner and mother of our three sons. I love you.

BOY SCOUTS OF AMERICA

The Boy Scouts of America has made a positive impact on the lives of millions of youth and adults. My long career in Scouting connects well with my roots of growing up on a farm. The codes of conduct shown below reflect the Scout principles and teachings.

Scout Oath

On my honor I will do my best
To do my duty to God and my country and to obey the Scout Law;
To help other people at all times;
To keep myself physically strong, mentally awake and morally straight.

Scout Law

A Scout is trustworthy, loyal, helpful, friendly, courteous, kind, obedient, cheerful, thrifty, brave, clean and reverent.

Motto

Be prepared.

Slogan

Do a good turn daily

ABOUT THE AUTHOR

Thomas R. Deimler was born on the second floor of his farm home on June 29, 1934. He lived there near Middletown, PA until his completion of high school.

Tom is a graduate of Penn State University, School of Forestry with a BS Degree in Wood Utilization Engineering. He later became a career professional with the Boy Scouts of America spanning some forty years.

In retirement, the past fifteen years, he has taught high school math part time and served as a substitute teacher.

Active in church and community, Tom continues his involvement of helping where needed.

He is married with three sons and eight grandchildren. Tom lives by the lessons of the land upon which he was raised. He has a strong religious faith and has dedicated his life to the service of others.

45203836R00089

Made in the USA
Charleston, SC
13 August 2015